# eat
## to the
# beat

edited by LISA SLATER

# eat
## to the
# beat

## a celebration of life and food

whitecap

Copy edited by Alison Maclean

Proofread by Viola Funk

Cover and interior design by Stacey Noyes / LuzForm Design

Recipes on pages 34 and 67 reprinted with permission of Lillian Kaplun / Baruna Group Inc.

Printed and bound in Canada

**National Library of Canada Cataloguing in Publication Data**

Eat to the beat

 Includes index.
 ISBN 1-55285-397-7

1. Cookery, Canadian.  I. Slater, Lisa.
TX715.6.E25 2002      641.5971      C2002-911008-4

The publisher acknowledges the support of the Canada Council for the Arts and the Cultural Services Branch of the Government of British Columbia for our publishing program. We acknowledge the financial support of the Government of Canada through the Book Publishing Industry Development Program for our publishing activities.

# Contents

## dedication

This book is dedicated to two groups of women: All those women past, present and future who have lived and died with breast cancer. All those women who have supported them, including and especially the founders, employees and volunteers of Willow.

## acknowledgments

This book would not have been possible without the unending support of a devoted group of women:

Many, many thanks, of course, to all the participating chefs.

Many, many thanks to our ever-loyal group of Eat to the Beat Committee volunteers, including and especially the year-after-year core:

My sister and co-founder of the event, Abigail Slater, Debra Rochman, Randi Hampson, and Sharon Hampson.

Many, many thanks to my family: parents, husband, children and sister's family who support me in everything that I attempt to do, including experimental meals which they have eaten without complaint but not without comment!

Last but not least: Thank you Alison Maclean, my editor, and Whitecap Books for seeing the potential for this book and acting on it.

# Foreword

In 1994, I was introduced to the idea of a breast cancer organization that would provide information and support to women diagnosed with breast cancer, using volunteers who themselves had dealt with that diagnosis. What a great idea ... but how does it move from idea to reality? Gather together for one brainstorming meeting a group of dynamic, devoted women, including some breast cancer survivors, and others equally concerned about the cause. This group of women were there long after that "only one meeting" and found the ideas and energy to eventually launch Willow, and to serve as its first board of directors.

In 1996, this same kind of collaboration gave birth to Eat to the Beat, the brainchild of Abigail and Lisa Slater and a most successful fund-raising event built around the talents and generosity of women chefs, bakers and caterers. How fitting that this wonderful cookbook, another example of women sharing their talents and expertise, should grow out of Eat to the Beat.

Finally, you the reader, by purchasing this cookbook, have made your contribution. As you enjoy these recipes and share the food with your family and friends, know that Willow and the community it serves are the grateful recipients of these collaborations.

Sharon Hampson, March 2002
(of Sharon, Lois and Bram)

# Willow

Willow Breast Cancer Support and Resource Services is a survivor-directed, non-profit organization that provides information and emotional support to individuals diagnosed with breast cancer, their families, friends and caregivers.

Founded in 1994, Willow is committed to serving a broad constituency including rural and urban communities across Canada, diverse ethnic and linguistic populations and people with disabilities. Willow ensures that breast cancer information and support are accessible to all through a variety of free services including a Canada-wide toll-free line, a comprehensive resource centre and service, an interactive Web site, training workshops, presentations to health care professionals concerning the psychosocial needs of their patients, and a support network program for over 70 self-help survivor groups.

For further information, please contact Willow:

> 785 Queen Street East
> Toronto, ON   M5M 1H5
> 416.778.5000 or
> toll-free at 1.888.778.3100
> www.willow.org

# Introduction

What is Eat to the Beat?

Eat to the Beat is an annual fundraising event that raises a good portion of the necessary operating funds for the Toronto-based Willow Breast Cancer Support and Resource Services. That statement alone is quite a mouthful as are the recipes in this cookbook!

Does the world need another cookbook? Perhaps. But as long as there are women diagnosed with breast cancer, the world needs Willow.

Willow was founded by, among others, a breast cancer survivor, Sharon Hampson of Sharon, Lois and Bram. She discovered when she was initially diagnosed that there was nowhere to get breast cancer information from women who had survived the gruelling and frightening treatments and yet had gone on to lead healthy, productive lives.

Willow, now in its eighth year of operation, has telephones staffed by breast cancer survivors, and provides treatment information to women newly diagnosed with the disease.

Eight years ago, when Willow launched its first fundraising event called the Launch of our Lives, my sister Abby attended. At the time, we ran a franchise company that donated a portion of its sales to charity. We had always provided product to almost any community organization that requested a donation, but now we sought to make a greater impact.

Instead, the impact was made on us. Abby returned from the event overwhelmed by the courage and strength of the women speakers, all of whom had survived breast cancer. In talking to our staff and friends we were shocked to learn of the many people, men and women, whose lives had been affected by someone with breast cancer.

I don't know why it came as such a surprise. My first mother-in-law died of it 25 years ago, but back then cancer was a word almost whispered, it was so frightening and almost embarrassing. As recently as eight years ago, though, even health professionals didn't have a place to send women and their families where they might arm themselves with information on treatment alternatives, discover local support groups, or speak one-on-one with survivors.

Abby and I asked Willow what we could do for them. The answer was immediate—help us raise money to supplement temporary government and corporate support.

We were delighted to help. We had long wanted to produce a spectacular food event that showcased pastry chefs because, as one myself, I felt that these behind-the-scenes professionals got short shrift when it came to publicity. (Many of us ran our own businesses and were not nearly as visible as some of the pioneers, like Dufflet, yet people ate our creations at fine restaurants, or purchased them at stores all around Toronto.) We wanted to place the spotlight on those women who worked in hotels and restaurants where the chef, usually a man, got the lion's share of attention and praise.

Eat to the Beat was born. A meeting was called, inviting a group of mostly independent, professional women bakers, some of whom had extensive experience in fundraising. We discussed the shape and structure of the event, the women that we might invite to participate, whether or not we should do a cookbook as well (no, was the decision!).

Abby and I assumed the lead and created a committee. The first Eat to the Beat took place at Casa Loma in 1995, during October, Breast Cancer Month. We had 20 pastry chefs offering incredible sweets, 350 guests, a $65 admission fee, a single corporate sponsor, and a silent auction. We raised about $75,000 for Willow.

Six years later, only three weeks after September 11, 2001, we raised over $200,000 with the help of two corporate sponsorships (one of which was the incredibly loyal and generous CIBC World Markets and its superwoman Susan Storey, who has supported us since day one), 650 guests who paid $125 per ticket, over 40 women chefs, 10 wineries and breweries, and 6 interior designers. Eat to the Beat had become one of the premier food and fundraising events in Toronto.

None of it would have been possible without the unending loyalty and enthusiasm of the women chefs themselves. Busy with their professional and private lives, they managed to elicit donations from their suppliers and provide superb food year after year, to an ever-increasing group of guests. They provided the food and the labour at no cost whatsoever to the event. It has clearly been a labour of love. And, amazingly, every year, we learned of yet another woman working in the back of some restaurant or food business, who should be included, and is invited. We can now claim over 60 women participants, from corporate chefs to individual caterers, from the most successful pastry chefs to struggling entrepreneurs.

And then of course, there was the Eat to the Beat Committee itself, consisting of an ever-changing group of dedicated women who found the time between careers and family to add one more activity to their already long list of things to do. Every single one of them helped us in large and small ways to make the event more successful.

Our success is also based on the consistent generosity of our donors, many of whom contributed when first asked seven years ago because they had been touched in some way by breast cancer. And yet, every year, we have to go out and ask again and again, for funds, for silent auction donations, for interior designers, for products and services that make our event possible. It is no easy task when there are so many other worthy causes and hard-working volunteers seeking the same kind of support.

Hence, our cookbook!

So, I repeat my initial question: Does the world really need another cookbook? Well, as long as there is a Willow and Willow requires operating funds, the world does, indeed, need another cookbook. Ten percent of the purchase price of this book goes directly to Willow.

You, gentle reader, wherever you may be, are getting a compilation of sensational recipes from most of the chefs who have participated in Eat to the Beat for the last six years. Once again, they pitched in during the busiest time of their year, to provide recipes in order for us to turn out a cookbook for our next event.

I have attempted to keep the recipes accessible, eliminating those with costly or hard to find ingredients, or techniques that would be difficult to execute in the home kitchen.

Perhaps the single most difficult thing in dealing with these contributing chefs was asking them to say something about themselves. Some asked me to do so, and I have. Most were reluctant to provide me with anything more than the barest information, while some, a very few, perhaps three in total, sent me press-release-like information in the third person that I have converted to the first person singular. Women, it seems, are still reluctant to trumpet their accomplishments. May this book do so on their behalf.

Bon appetit!

# About the weights and measures ...

It is no small feat to wrestle over 150 recipes from 40 chefs into a single, comprehensible and user-friendly, whole.

Every author has a different style; some assumed that I would know how to finish their recipes when they ran out of time to complete them; some sent me restaurant quantities that, in testing, left me with weeks' worth of a single dish which, albeit delicious, was hard to consume in a household of two! Others provided me with imperial measurements, some with weight, and not enough, alas, with metric.

As a result, in order to make this book useful not only to the passionate amateur, but to professionals as well, I had to establish certain guidelines.

Every recipe has both imperial and metric measures.

1   Most of the measurements for things like chopped onions, raisins, sweet peppers, etc. are based on my own averaging and production. I followed the recipe, produced the ingredients, and weighed and measured as I went along in an attempt to standardize the recipes. One woman's medium onion is another's small, and 4 chicken breasts can vary from 4 oz (112 g) to 6 oz (170 g).

2   Where I felt the weight wasn't particularly important, as in chicken breasts, for example, I left it in the author's original specification either in units or weight.

3   Converting from imperial to metric isn't problematic if one wants to be precise: 6 oz translates into 168 g, but 168 g, while possible to weigh on digital scale, is difficult if not impossible on a balance scale. So, whenever the rounding of metric wouldn't, in my view, wildly affect the taste or the result of the dish, I round up to the nearest 5 or 10.

4    Where rounding up might affect an outcome, as it could in baking, I either left it in the original form specified, or in the exact metric conversion with no rounding up.

About the ingredients …

1    Use the best quality you can afford.

2    Cook and purchase with the seasons for maximum flavor and minimum cost.

3    Purchase organic whenever possible because it's not only good for you, it's good for our planet.

In the recipes

All eggs are large.

All butter is unsalted.

Sugar is granulated unless otherwise noted.

Adjust flavors and seasoning to suit your taste.

# chapter 1

# desserts

"Life is short. Eat dessert first!"

Eat to the Beat's first event consisted of 20 women pastry chefs strutting their stuff, much of it chocolate! Imagine 350 guests roaming the majestic rooms of Toronto's castle on the hill, Casa Loma, with drinks in hand, trying to decide how not to miss a single dessert. The only complaint after the first year was: too many desserts!

Frankly, we feel you can never have too many desserts, so we decided to start our cookbook in the same way we started the event: with desserts, in order to showcase the tremendous variety and skills of both well- and not-so-well-known women culinary professionals. Some are primarily pastry chefs, while others you will see contributing to later chapters in the book.

Everything is represented here, from the most basic brownies to the most sophisticated millefeuilles. But don't feel daunted: all the recipes are easily do-able at home and will yield great results.

There is a remarkable number of fruit desserts, from apples to persimmon, as well as an unusual number of desserts showcasing caramel or toffee. Of course, we couldn't do a book without classic chocolate favorites, so here they are, from chocolate cakes to truffles.

This chapter will keep you busy, and your family and friends happy, for a long, long time.

Enjoy!

Linda Haynes
**Ace Bakery**

"This is pure comfort food. It also looks spectacular and tastes heavenly. You could make the fruit compote the day before, bring it to room temperature before spooning it into the tin and bake it while you're getting dinner ready. The Crème Anglaise will keep in the fridge for 3 to 4 days, so it can be made ahead, too."

# Apple, Pear and Cranberry Charlotte
## with Crème Anglaise

2 Tbsp unsalted butter 30 g

6 cups Bosc pears 6 large peeled and cored, cut in 1-inch (2.5-cm) pieces

6 cups Spy apples 4 large peeled and cored, cut in 1-inch (2.5-cm) pieces

1 piece star anise 1 piece

½ vanilla bean ½ split

1 tsp lemon juice 5 mL

2 Tbsp sugar 25 g

4 Tbsp maple syrup 60 mL

⅔ cup dried cranberries 85 g

2 tsp dry sherry 10 mL

1 scant tsp grated orange rind 4 mL

⅔ cup melted unsalted butter 160 mL

16-20 slices white bread 16-20 slices crusts removed

Crème Anglaise (pp 19-20) or vanilla ice cream

**Serves 6**

Melt 2 Tbsp (30 g) butter in a frying pan large enough to hold all the fruit.

Add pears, apples, star anise, vanilla bean and lemon juice. Cook over medium heat for 3-4 minutes, stirring occasionally.

Add sugar and maple syrup and cook for another 5 minutes, stirring occasionally or until the juice is almost all evaporated but the fruit still holds its shape. Remove from heat.

Add the cranberries, sherry, and orange rind.

When the mixture is cool, scrape the seeds from the vanilla bean into the compote and remove the star anise. You should have about 6 cups (1.5 L) of fruit.

Preheat oven to 375°F (190°C).

Brush one side of each piece of bread with melted butter.

Line the bottom of an 8-cup (2 L) charlotte tin with overlapping triangles of bread.

Brush lightly with more butter.

Cut the rest of the bread slices vertically and line the side of the pan, butter side out against the pan, over-lapping the pieces of bread.

Fill the middle of the tin with the fruit, pressing against the bread.

Cover the top of the mold with overlapping slices of bread and brush with remaining butter.

Place in the oven and bake for 40 minutes.

Check after 20 minutes to make sure the top is not over-browning. If it is, cover loosely with foil.

Remove from the oven and set aside for 10 minutes.

Place a plate on top of the mold and, holding both the plate and the mold, invert onto the plate.

Dust with icing sugar and pour the Crème Anglaise around the edge of the plate. Serve warm.

Catherine O'Donnell

Pastry Chef
Hillebrand
Vineyard Café

"At the age of 14, I visited Toronto's King Edward Hotel for afternoon tea and thus began a love affair with baking. The experience led me to enroll in George Brown College to study in the Pastry Arts Program. In addition to numerous awards, and a place on the College's Culinary Team, I was named one of Canada's Top Culinary Students. After school it was off to Europe, where I studied at the Callebaut Institute in Belgium. Returning home, I honed my talents as the Executive Pastry Chef of the King Edward Hotel, and the Pastry Chef for Vintage Inns of Niagara-on-the-Lake. I joined Hillebrand's Vineyard Café as the pastry chef in 1999."

# Apple Coffee Cake
## with Butterscotch Sauce

1 ½ cups vegetable oil 375 mL

2 cups sugar 400 g

3 eggs 150 g

2 cups bread flour 260 g

1 cup whole wheat flour 145 g

¾ tsp baking soda 3 mL

¼ tsp salt 1 mL

¼ tsp cinnamon 1 mL

pinch cloves pinch

pinch mace pinch

3 cups (2 medium) apples 335 g
    peeled and chopped

1 cup pecans 90 g
    toasted, chopped (optional)


### Butterscotch Sauce

1 cup brown sugar 220 g

2 Tbsp cornstarch 15 g

pinch salt pinch

2 Tbsp unsalted butter 30 g

1 ¼ cups cold water 315 mL

1 tsp vanilla 5 mL

¼ cup brandy 65 mL


**16 servings**

Preheat oven to 325°F (160°C). Grease a 9-inch x 13-inch (23-cm x 33-cm) baking pan with vegetable spray.

In the bowl of an electric mixer fitted with the paddle attachment, place the oil, sugar and eggs. On medium speed, mix to blend completely.

Meanwhile, mix all the dry ingredients together with a fork.

Turn mixer to low and gradually add dry ingredients. Mix only enough to incorporate completely.

Remove bowl from mixer and add apples and, if using, pecans, folding them in by hand.

Pour batter into prepared pan and spread evenly with an offset spatula.

Bake for approximately 1 hour or until the center is puffed, firm to the touch and a toothpick tests clean.

Serve warm with Butterscotch Sauce and whipped cream.


### Butterscotch Sauce

In a medium saucepan set over high heat, combine brown sugar, cornstarch, salt and butter.

Stir until brown sugar starts to melt and turns slightly brown.

Add cold water. Reduce heat and cook until mixture starts to thicken.

Remove from heat and add vanilla and brandy.

Store in fridge until ready to use. Warm in a saucepan or microwave before serving.

Joanne Yolles
Freelance Pastry Chef

"This is a sophisticated dessert I originally developed for a California winery using their late harvest Riesling. Naturally, any of the Niagara late harvest Rieslings would be equally delicious. The only sugar in the filling is the sugar occurring in the wine and the apples."

# Caramelized Millefeuilles
## with a Compote of Apples, Late Harvest Riesling, and Golden Raisins

⅓ cup golden raisins 45 g

¾ to 1 cup late harvest Riesling 185-250 mL

1 ½ lbs puff pastry 750 g

4 large Spy apples 1 kg
    peeled and cored

### Vanilla Bean Crème Anglaise

1 ½ cups milk 375 mL

½ cup 35% whipping cream 125 mL

⅓ cup sugar 85 g

½ vanilla bean ½
    split

5 egg yolks 5

8 servings

Combine the raisins and 1/2 cup (125 mL) of the late harvest Riesling in a small bowl. Let stand at room temperature overnight.

Line two 12-inch x 15-inch (30-cm x 38-cm) baking pans with parchment paper.

Roll out the puff pastry to 1/8 inch (.3 cm) thick and large enough to line the baking pans.

Chill for at least 1 hour.

Preheat oven to 425°F (220°C).

Prick the dough generously with a fork and cover with another sheet of parchment paper. Set a second baking pan on top of the parchment-covered pastry to weigh down the dough.

Bake for 10-15 minutes, pricking the dough again if necessary to prevent it from rising.

Just when pastry is browning, and appears to be set, remove top baking sheet and parchment paper, reduce oven to 375°F (190°C), and continue baking pastry until it is golden and crisp.

Remove from the oven and cool on a wire rack.

Trim the edges using a serrated knife and cut into rectangles approximately 2 inches x 3 1/2 inches (5 cm x 9 cm)—you should have 24 in all.

Check the raisins. They should be very plump and soft. If necessary, simmer over gentle heat to soften a little further.

Drain the raisins, reserving the liquid. Measure the liquid and add more wine to equal 3/4 cup (185 mL).

continued

# Caramelized Millefeuilles (continued)

Cut the apples into 1/2-inch (1.2-cm) pieces.

Combine wine and apples in a wide skillet.

Cook without covering, stirring every few minutes with a wooden spoon until apples have reduced and liquid has evaporated. The compote should be thick with tender pieces of apple throughout—do not mash or purée.

Remove from the heat and fold in the raisins.

Assemble the dessert while the compote is warm. It can be made ahead and gently reheated.

Vanilla Bean Crème Anglaise

Combine milk, cream, and sugar in a medium saucepan.

Scrape the black seeds from the vanilla bean into milk mixture and then add the bean.

Scald the milk mixture on high heat just until tiny bubbles appear around the edges.

In a separate bowl, whisk the egg yolks and very gradually pour in the heated milk mixture in a slow stream, whisking constantly.

Pour the custard back into the saucepan and set over moderate heat.

Using a wooden spoon, stir slowly and continuously until the custard thickens enough to coat the back of the spoon. Do not allow the custard to heat past a simmer.

Place a fine sieve over a medium bowl and strain the Crème Anglaise.

Cool to room temperature, then refrigerate until ready to serve.

| | |
|---|---|
| Assembly | Place a piece of baked pastry on a serving plate. |
| | Spread a layer of apple compote on the pastry. Top with a second layer of pastry, a layer of apples, and a third layer of pastry. |
| | Continue assembling the millefeuilles with the remaining pastry and apples. |
| | Sift icing sugar generously over the top of each mille-feuille. |
| | Place under the broiler for a few moments or until the sugar has melted and caramelized. |
| | Serve immediately with Crème Anglaise. |

Joanne Yolles
Freelance Pastry
Chef

# Fresh Apricot and Hazelnut Tart

## Tart Shell

1 ¼ cups + 2 Tbsp all-purpose flour
  175 g

¼ cup sugar 50 g

½ cup unsalted butter 112 g
  cut into ½-inch (1.2-cm) cubes

1 egg yolk 1

2 Tbsp 35% whipping cream 30 mL

## Filling

½ cup unsalted butter 112 g
  room temperature

½ cup + 3 Tbsp sugar 130 g

2 eggs 2

½ tsp vanilla 2 mL

1 cup ground hazelnuts 120 g
  lightly toasted*

3 Tbsp all-purpose flour 20 g

¾ cup apricot jam 190 mL

15-20 ripe apricots 15-20

**8 servings**

## Tart Shell

Place flour and sugar in the bowl of a food processor fitted with the steel blade. Pulse to combine.

Add butter and process to a cornmeal-like consistency.

In a small bowl, combine the egg yolk and cream and, with the machine running, add to flour mixture. Stop the machine as soon as dough begins to come together.

Turn the dough out onto work surface and work it gently with your hands until it comes together. If the dough seems a little dry or crumbly, add a few more drops of cream.

The dough can be rolled immediately if it is not too soft. If necessary, wrap in plastic wrap and chill for about 1 hour. Alternatively, the dough can be pressed right into the pan after it is made.

On a lightly floured surface, roll the dough about 1/8 inch (.3 cm) thick and 12 inches (30 cm) in diameter. Line a 10-inch (25-cm) tart pan with a removable bottom. Chill the tart shell for at least 1 hour.

Preheat oven to 375°F (190°C).

Line the whole interior of the shell with aluminum foil and fill with dry beans or pie weights.

Bake for 15-20 minutes or until the pastry is dry and set around the edges.

Remove the beans and foil, prick the bottom of the pastry with a fork and bake 15-20 minutes longer until the pastry is fully baked and golden brown.

Cool the tart shell on a wire rack before proceeding.

*Ground hazelnuts can be purchased in specialty stores or made by grinding in your food processor, being careful not to over-process. Sift to remove larger pieces and process them again until finely ground. To toast, preheat oven to 300°F (150°C) and spread the nuts on a parchment-lined cooking sheet. Toast, stirring occasionally until golden and fragrant, about 10 minutes. Watch them carefully. Alternatively, you can toast whole hazelnuts, remove their skin and process them with the flour until they are powdery without being oily.

Filling

Preheat oven to 375°F (190°C).

In the bowl of an electric mixer fitted with the paddle attachment, cream the butter and 1/2 cup (100 g) sugar until combined.

Add eggs 1 at a time, beating well after each addition. Add vanilla. Beat until smooth.

With the machine on low speed, add the ground hazel-nuts and flour, beating just until they are combined with the butter and eggs.

Spread 1/3 cup (85 mL) of the apricot jam on the bottom of the pre-baked tart shell. Spoon the hazelnut mixture into the shell and spread evenly.

Cut apricots in half and remove pits. If apricots are large, cut into quarters.

Arrange in concentric circles, cut side up, on hazelnut filling. Sprinkle with the remaining granulated sugar.

Bake the tart for 50 minutes or until the filling puffs and is golden brown. Remove the tart from the oven and cool on a wire rack.

In a small saucepan set over low heat, warm the remaining apricot jam with 2 tsp (10 mL) water, stirring constantly to thin. Strain the jam through a fine sieve. Discard the solids (or put back into the jar of jam and use on bread).

Brush the tart with the strained jam.

Serve warm or at room temperature with lightly sweetened whipped cream or vanilla ice cream.

Daphna
Rabinovitch
*Canadian Living*
Magazine

"This is one of my personal favorites. It's great for a brunch or a weekend luncheon. It's moist and flavorful and best eaten the same day. Try to buy the small wild blueberries, but if you can't, try using fresh or frozen raspberries instead."

# Blueberry Cheese Coffee Cake

### Crumb Topping

1 cup all-purpose flour 140 g

¼ cup brown sugar 55 g

¼ cup sugar 50 g

½ tsp cinnamon 2 mL

⅓ cup unsalted butter 75 g
melted

### Cheese Filling

8 oz cream cheese 227 g

¼ cup sugar 50 g

1 egg 1

1 tsp finely grated lemon rind 5 mL

### Batter

⅓ cup unsalted butter 75 g
softened

2 eggs 2

2 tsp vanilla 10 mL

1 ½ cups all-purpose flour 210 g

1 tsp baking powder 5 mL

1 tsp baking soda 5 mL

¼ tsp salt 1 mL

½ cup light sour cream 125 mL

1 ½ cups wild blueberries 210 mL
fresh or frozen

**8 servings**

### Crumb Topping

In a small bowl, combine flour, both sugars, and cinnamon. Drizzle butter evenly over top. Toss until thoroughly moistened. Set aside.

### Cheese Filling

In the bowl of an electric mixer fitted with the paddle attachment, beat the cream cheese with the sugar until light and fluffy, scraping down sides of bowl.

Beat in the egg and the lemon rind just until smooth. Set aside.

### Batter

Preheat oven to 350°F (180°C). Grease a 9-inch (23-cm) springform pan with vegetable spray.

In the bowl of an electric mixer fitted with the paddle attachment, beat the butter with the sugar until well combined. Beat in eggs, one at a time, beating well and scraping after each addition. Add vanilla. Remove from the mixer.

In a separate bowl, combine flour, baking powder, baking soda and salt.

Using a wooden spoon, stir the flour into the butter mixture alternately with the sour cream in three additions, mixing thoroughly but gently.

Spread the batter evenly in the prepared pan, mounding it slightly in the center.

**Batter**
continued

Sprinkle 2/3 cup (160 mL) of the blueberries overtop.

Gently spread cream cheese filling over the blueberries.

Sprinkle with remaining blueberries.

Sprinkle crumb topping over blueberries.

Bake for about 1 hour and 15 minutes or until the edges are set and just beginning to come away from the sides of the pan. Let cool in pan on a wire rack for 30 minutes. Serve warm or at room temperature.

Wanda Beaver

**Wanda's Pie
in the Sky**

"This is the first pie I ever baked, made from cherries picked in my own back yard. I was just nine years old and yes, it is still my favorite. Sour cherries are the ideal fruit for a pie—juicy, intensely flavored and gorgeous to look at.

"Sour cherry season is short but you can find them in the supermarkets and in farmers' markets during the summer. Purchase large buckets of already frozen Niagara cherries so you can enjoy the taste of summer all winter long!"

# Ontario Sour Cherry Pie

**Pie Dough**

2 ½ cups all-purpose flour 350 g

¼ tsp salt 1.25 mL

½ cup cold unsalted butter 112 g
  cubed

½ cup frozen shortening 112 g
  cubed

⅓ cup cold water 80 mL


**Cherry Pie Filling**

1 egg 1

1 Tbsp water 15 mL

6 ½ cups sour cherries 1.6 L
  pitted, fresh or frozen

1 cup sugar 200 g
  or more to taste

3 Tbsp cornstarch 25 g

½ tsp almond extract 2 mL

1 Tbsp sugar 14 g


8 servings

Make sure all the dough ingredients are as cold as possible.

Using a food processor fitted with the steel blade or a pastry cutter, combine the flour, salt, butter and shortening. Process or cut into the mixture until it is the consistency of coarse meal and begins to clump together.

Sprinkle water over the mix and allow to rest 30 seconds.

Process very briefly or cut with about 15 strokes of the pastry cutter just until the ingredients come away from the sides of the bowl.

Remove dough from the bowl and form into a cylinder. Divide the cylinder into a two thirds and one third piece. Flatten each into a disc, cover with plastic wrap and refrigerate for at least 20 minutes.

Fifteen minutes prior to rolling, remove the dough from the fridge.

Make the egg wash by mixing the egg with the water and set aside.

On a lightly floured surface, roll the larger disc into a circle 1/8 inch (.3 cm) thick and 13 inches (32 cm) across.

Gently fold the dough in half and place it in the middle of the pie plate. Unfold the dough, and press it into the bottom and sides. Turn the overhanging pastry under itself to create an even edge 1/2 inch (1.25 cm) beyond the rim of the 9-inch (23-cm) pie plate.

In a large bowl mix together the cherries, sugar, cornstarch and almond extract.

Let sit for a few minutes so that the cornstarch can absorb some of the cherry juice.

Toss cherries once again and pour into prepared pie shell. Be sure to mound them in the center and somewhat away from the edges to allow for the top crust and the crimped edges of the pie.

On a lightly floured surface, roll out the remaining disc of dough into a circle 1/8 inch (.3 cm) thick.

Using a knife or a decorative crimping cutter, cut the round into fourteen 3/4-inch (1.9-cm) strips.

With the leftover dough scraps, cut out freehand or with a cookie cutter, three 1-inch (2.5-cm) cherries, three 2-inch x 1/8-inch (5-cm x .3-cm) cherry stems and two 2-inch (5-cm) leaves.

Brush the rim of the pie crust lightly with water.

Weave a lattice crust over the top of the pie using the strips. Gently press the point where the strips meet the crust.

When the lattice is complete, trim the strips even with the bottom pie crust.

Crimp the outside edges of the pie crust by placing the thumb and forefinger of your left hand against the outside of the overhanging pie crust and push in from the inside using your right forefinger to create a V-shape.

Decide where you are going to place the cherry cut-outs and brush the area lightly with water. Place the cut-outs to resemble 3 cherries joined into 2 leaves.

Brush lattice with egg wash and sprinkle with remaining 1 Tbsp (10 g) sugar.

At this point, it is preferable, but not critical, for the pie to chill for 30 minutes.

Bake the pie for 10 minutes at 400°F (200°C) and then reduce temperature to 350°F (180°C).

Bake 50-60 minutes or until the crust is golden and filling is bubbling in the center.

Serve slightly warm or at room temperature.

Sandy Kaminker
**Freelance Pastry Chef/Caterer**

"Passionate" is how pastry chef/caterer Sandy Kaminker describes her relationship with baking. She has been baking small, elegant cookies, fine tortes, and pastries for several years and that passion is evident in every piece that bears her signature. Sandy trained in the US with Albert Kumin, former White House pastry chef, and has studied with Betty Norstrand (a former US Culinary Olympic team participant) as well as Rose Levy Berenbaum (author of the best-selling *The Cake Bible*). She has taught baking all over Toronto.

# Passover Date Bars

### Topping

½ cup matzoh cake meal 70 g
(or all-purpose flour)

⅓ cup brown sugar 75 g

4 Tbsp unsalted butter 56 g

½ cup chopped pecans 60 g

### Crust

1 cup matzoh cake meal 140 g
(or all-purpose flour)

⅓ cup brown sugar 75 g

pinch salt pinch

¾ tsp cinnamon 3 mL

5 Tbsp unsalted butter 70 g

1 egg yolk 50 mL
mixed with 2 Tbsp (30 mL) ice water

½ tsp vanilla 2 mL

### Filling

3 cups honey dates 600 g
(approximately)

1 cup orange juice 250 mL

¼-½ cup water 65-125 mL

2 oranges 2
rind finely grated

2 Tbsp fresh lemon juice 30 mL

1 Tbsp brandy 15 mL

2 tsp vanilla 10 mL

**16 bars**

### Topping

In the bowl of a food processor fitted with the steel blade, process all the ingredients just until crumbly. Set aside.

### Crust

Preheat oven to 350°F (180°C). Line an 8-inch (20-cm) square baking pan with parchment paper.

In the bowl of a food processor fitted with the steel blade, blend cake meal (or flour), sugar, salt, and cinnamon.

Add butter and pulse briefly to work the butter into the dry ingredients until it resembles coarse meal.

Add the vanilla to the egg/water mixture.

With the motor running, pour the liquid ingredients into the bowl. Process just until dry ingredients are moistened.

Press into the prepared pan.

Chill in fridge for at least 30 minutes.

Bake for 15 minutes. Cool 5 to 10 minutes before filling.

### Filling

In a heavy-bottomed saucepan over medium heat mix dates, orange juice, water and orange rind.

Cook on medium-low heat until dates are tender, 15-20 minutes. If mixture becomes dry during cooking, add a little more water.

Mash with a fork or place in a food processor and purée until smooth.

Add lemon juice, brandy and vanilla. Cool.

Preheat oven to 350°F (180°C).

| | |
|---|---|
| Assembly | Spread date purée over cooled crust. |
| | Crumble topping evenly over date filling. |
| | Bake for 35-40 minutes. |
| | Cool completely before placing a cutting board over the date bars and flipping them over. Remove the pan. Place a second cutting board on the upside-down bars and flip over again. |
| | Cut into bars. Store in fridge for up to 3 days or in freezer, well wrapped, for 3 months. |
| | |
| Editor's Note | The Jewish holiday of Passover, with its strict dietary restrictions regarding the consumption of wheat, among other things, is particularly challenging. The recipes presented in this chapter, for example, are easily adapted by substituting matzoh meal for flour, non-dairy margarine for butter and non-dairy whipped topping for whipped cream. |

Anne Yarymowich

**The Agora at the
Art Gallery of Ontario**

"My most memorable experience with Tarte Tatin is one that I like to tell to apprentices, or cooks who have just made a serious blunder. Donna Dooher, the owner of Mildred Pierce Restaurant, was expecting her mother for lunch with a group of twenty women. Tarte Tatin was to be the dessert. Three pans with sugar in each were set on the burners. Why didn't the sugar caramelize? Then I realized in haste, I had taken 'sugar' from the salt bin!"

# Tarte Tatin

### Pie Dough

2 cups all-purpose flour 280 g

pinch salt pinch

8 Tbsp unsalted butter 112 g

8 Tbsp vegetable shortening 112 g

¼ cup + 1 Tbsp ice cold water 80 g

Yield 2, 10-inch (25-cm) pie shells


### Tarte Tatin Apple Filling

1 cup sugar 200 g

3 Tbsp water 45 mL

2 Tbsp unsalted butter 30 g

7 cooking apples 1.5 kg
  peeled cored and quartered

½ recipe pie dough 275 g


8 servings

Place flour in a medium bowl.

With a cheese grater, grate butter and shortening into flour.

Work the flour and fat together quickly with your fingertips until it resembles oatmeal.

Add water all at once, incorporating with hands only until dough comes together. Do not over work.

Shape into a round, flat disc. Wrap in plastic and chill for about 10 minutes. Or freeze for up to 3 months wrapped in plastic and foil.


Tarte Tatin Apple Filling

Preheat oven to 350°F (180°C).

Place sugar and water in a heavy-bottomed 10-inch (25-cm) frying pan on high heat.

Roll out pie dough to between 1/8 inch (.3 cm) and 1/4 inch (.6 cm) thick and 11 inches (28 cm) in diameter.

When the sugar begins to caramelize, allow it to go to a golden brown then remove from heat and add butter. Swirl it around to combine.

Arrange apple quarters, rounded side down, over sugar (about 10 pieces around the sides, 3 or 4 in the center).

Cover apples with rolled pie dough. Fold any overhanging dough over top of dough.

Bake for 15-20 minutes or until the pie dough is golden brown.

Have an 11-inch (28-cm) or 12-inch (30-cm) plate ready to place over the hot pie. Hold the plate firmly in one hand while you invert the pan onto the plate.

Serve immediately.

Izabela Kalabis
Chef
Inniskillin Wines

"I confess to absolutely loving sweets. In fact, I will often skip a course to make sure I have room for dessert. This recipe was developed for Inniskillin to marry with icewine, and I have to admit I was thrilled with the union. The steps are numerous, although well worth the effort. If you prefer, the coulis can be omitted with little sacrifice to taste; however, it does add to the presentation."

# Icewine Soaked Figs on Hazelnut Crust
## with White Chocolate Mousse, Icewine Sabayon and Raspberry Coulis

### Hazelnut Crust

3 egg whites 3

1 Tbsp sugar 15 g

½ cup ground hazelnuts 60 g (p 22)

½ cup icing sugar 60 g

1 Tbsp flour 9 g sifted

### White Chocolate Mousse

¼ lb white chocolate 115 g coarsely chopped

1 gelatin sheet 2 g

1 egg 1

⅔ cup 35% whipped cream 160 mL

### Figs in Icewine

1 Tbsp unsalted butter 15 g

4 ripe figs 4

½ cup icewine 125 mL

### Raspberry Coulis

1 cup fresh raspberries 150 g

1-2 Tbsp sugar 15-30 g

### Sabayon

2 egg yolks 2

1 Tbsp sugar 15 g

¼ cup icewine 60 mL

**4 servings**

### Hazelnut Crust

Preheat oven to 300°F (150°C). Line a baking sheet with parchment paper.

Trace four 4-inch (10-cm) circles on the paper and flip over. Set aside.

In the bowl of an electric mixer fitted with the whisk attachment, beat the egg whites until soft peak stage.

Gradually add sugar and beat for another minute. Stop the mixer.

Mix together ground hazelnuts and icing sugar.

Remove bowl from mixer and, using a rubber spatula, fold in the hazelnuts, icing sugar and flour. Do not overmix.

Fit a piping bag with a 1/4-inch (.6-cm) plain piping tube. Pour the hazelnut meringue batter into the bag and, starting at the center of a traced circle, pipe the batter in a spiral out to the edge. Continue with remaining traced circles.

Bake for about 1 hour or until dry. Set aside. If not using immediately, store in an airtight container.

### White Chocolate Mousse

In a small bowl set over a pot of barely simmering water, place the white chocolate. Melt partially and remove from heat, allowing the residual heat in the chocolate to melt the rest.

Meanwhile, immerse the sheet of gelatin in cold water to soften. It will take about 3 minutes.

continued

# Icewine Soaked Figs on Hazelnut Crust

(continued)

**White Chocolate Mousse**
continued

Put the egg in a small saucepan and place it over low heat, whisking briskly until it is frothy and very warm. Remove from the heat.

Squeeze all the water from the gelatin and add to the egg, whisking to melt the gelatin. Add melted chocolate and whisk to incorporate all the ingredients.

Fold in whipped cream. Refrigerate until set, about 2 hours.

**Figs in Icewine**

Place butter in a saucepan large enough to hold all the ingredients.

Add figs and cook for a few minutes over medium heat, turning figs gently from time to time.

Add icewine and continue cooking until wine evaporates and figs are slightly caramelized. Set aside.

**Raspberry Coulis**

In the bowl of a food processor fitted with the steel blade, purée the raspberries and sugar.

Strain to remove the seeds.

Taste to make sure it is not too tart, but don't make it too sweet, either.

**Sabayon**

Right before serving, prepare the Sabayon.

In a medium bowl set over a pot of barely simmering water, place all the ingredients.

Whisk briskly until thick and foamy, being careful not to scramble the eggs.

**Assembly**

Place a dollop of White Chocolate Mousse on top of each hazelnut crust.

Cut a deep cross in the top of each fig to open it up. Place 1 fig on top of the mousse.

Drizzle some Sabayon on top of the mousse and around the plate.

Surround the assembled dessert with Raspberry Coulis.

**Editor's Note**

As with most multi-stepped recipes, this one can be broken down into less demanding steps by starting assembly a few days before the dessert is needed. Best of all, you will feel like a chef in doing so!

Lillian Kaplun

Mentor / Cooking
Teacher /
Cookbook Author

"The best way to become an expert dessert-maker is through experience. You'll learn how ingredients like egg whites can act differently according to the weather, how your oven can have an individual personality, and even how the temperature of your hands can affect your pastry. Be patient with yourself and when you're baking, be precise. The outcome depends on specific chemical interactions, so accuracy counts.

"Provide yourself with the right equipment—plenty of mixing bowls, measuring cups and spoons, and the best electric mixer you can afford."

# Lemon Chiffon Cake

2 ¼ cups cake flour 270 g
   sifted

1 cup sugar 200 g

1 Tbsp baking powder 12 g

1 tsp salt 5 mL

5 egg yolks 5

⅓ cup vegetable oil 80 mL

¾ cup water 185 mL

2 tsp fresh lemon juice 10 mL

2 tsp vanilla 10 mL

1 lemon 1
   rind finely grated

1 ¼ cups egg whites 315 mL

½ tsp cream of tartar 2 mL

½ cup sugar 100 g

**10-12 servings**

Preheat oven to 325°F (160°C). Have ready an ungreased 10-inch (25-cm) tube pan.

Sift together flour, 1 cup (200 g) sugar, baking powder and salt into the bowl of an electric mixer.

Make a well in the center. Add egg yolks, oil, water, juice, vanilla, and lemon rind.

In the bowl of an electric mixer fitted with the whisk attachment, beat egg whites on medium speed. When they become frothy, add cream of tartar.

Increase the speed and add 1/2 cup (100 g) of sugar and beat to a meringue consistency of stiff, but not dry, peaks.

While beating the egg whites, stir the egg yolk mixture with a spoon.

When whites are removed from electric mixer, beat the egg yolk mixture using the same whisk attachment, for 1 minute or until smooth.

Fold the egg yolk mixture into the egg white mixture gradually, blending well.

Pour batter into ungreased tube pan. Cut through batter quickly with a spatula to clear air bubbles.

Bake for 55 minutes.

Increase oven to 350°F (180°C) and bake for 15 minutes longer.

Invert onto a small but sturdy glass.

Cool for at least 1 hour.

Remove from pan and store.

Dufflet Rosenberg
Dufflet Pastries

"Any of us who grew up in the '70s remembers the mystique of 'Baked Alaska.' Problem was, all too often these pyrotechnical events resulted in nothing more than a trashy brick of Neapolitan ice cream cleverly disguised under a blanket of meringue.

"For my 'haute' take on this kitschy classic—kind of lemon meringue pie meets the freezer—you must make your own Lemon Custard Ice Cream. No substitutes allowed! It's easy to make, fun to flambé and you'll impress your friends and family … suddenly I'm sounding like a '70s K-Tel commercial!"

# Individual Baked Alaskas

### Almond Sponge Sheet

7 eggs 7

1 ½ cups sugar 300 g

1 ⅔ cups ground almonds 140 g

¼ tsp salt 1 mL

icing sugar

### Lemon Custard Ice Cream

3 lemons 3
    rind finely grated

½ cup freshly squeezed lemon juice
    125 mL

¾ cup sugar 150 g

2 cups 10% cream 500 mL

4 egg yolks 4

pinch salt pinch

2 cups 35% whipping cream 500 mL

### 6 servings

### Almond Sponge Sheet

Preheat oven to 400°F (200°C).

Line a 16-inch x 12-inch (30-cm x 40-cm) baking pan with parchment paper, leaving a 1-inch (2.5-cm) overhang.

Place the eggs and sugar in the bowl of an electric mixer fitted with the whisk attachment.

Beat until very thick and pale in color.

Remove the bowl from the mixer.

Combine the almonds and the salt and gently fold into the eggs with a balloon whisk or rubber spatula.

Spread the batter into the prepared pan and bake until golden brown, 8-9 minutes.

Transfer to a wire rack to cool.

Sprinkle with icing sugar and turn out onto parchment paper.

### Lemon Custard Ice Cream

In a small bowl, combine the lemon rind and juice.

Stir in the sugar and let the mixture stand for at least 30 minutes.

In a medium saucepan, bring the 10% cream just to the boil over medium heat.

Meanwhile, combine the egg yolks and the salt to blend.

Whisking constantly, slowly add about 1/2 cup (125 mL) of the hot cream to the yolks and mix until completely incorporated.

continued

# Individual Baked Alaskas (continued)

## Assembly

½ cup icing sugar 60 g

## Blueberry Sauce

2 cups wild blueberries 500 g
    fresh or frozen

¼ cup sugar 50 g

2 Tbsp fresh lemon juice 30 g

1 lemon 1
    rind grated

¼ cup water 65 mL

1 Tbsp cornstarch 15 mL

2-3 Tbsp orange liqueur 30-45 mL

## Meringue

4 egg whites 4

½ tsp cream of tartar 2 mL

pinch salt pinch

1 cup sugar 200 g

1 tsp vanilla 5 mL

Return the egg mixture to the pan with the hot cream.

Cook the custard over medium heat, stirring constantly, until it is thick enough to coat the back of a wooden spoon. Do not let it boil or it will curdle.

As soon as it reaches the proper consistency, immediately remove from the heat and strain through a fine sieve into a bowl.

Stir in the lemon mixture and the whipping cream.

Cover with plastic and chill completely.

Pour into an ice cream maker and freeze according to manufacturer's instructions.

Freeze finished ice cream in a covered container until ready to use.

### Assembly

If the ice cream is very firm, let it soften slightly in the refrigerator, about 30 minutes.

Meanwhile, line six 3/4-cup (185-mL) molds or custard cups with plastic wrap.

Cut out six 4-inch (10-cm) circles from the almond cake and use these to line the bottom and sides of the molds. Set aside the remaining cake to use as bottoms. If the cake seems sticky, dip your fingers into the icing sugar.

Pack the molds with the lemon ice cream.

Cut or piece together remaining cake to cover the bottoms of the molds.

Freeze for at least 30 minutes or wrap with plastic and keep frozen until ready to finish and serve.

| | |
|---|---|
| Blueberry Sauce | In a medium saucepan, combine the berries, sugar, lemon juice and rind, and half the water. |
| | Cook over medium heat, stirring until the sugar is dissolved and berries release their juice. |
| | Dissolve the cornstarch into the remaining water and stir into the blueberries. |
| | Bring to a boil and continue boiling for 1 minute until the sauce is thickened and clear. |
| | Taste. Add liqueur and more sugar if necessary. |
| | Store in the refrigerator. |
| Meringue | Place the egg whites in the bowl of an electric mixer fitted with the whisk attachment and beat until frothy. |
| | Add the cream of tartar and the salt and slowly add the sugar. |
| | Beat until stiff but not dry. |
| | Beat in the vanilla. |
| Final Assembly | Remove the Baked Alaskas from their molds and arrange on a parchment-lined baking pan. |
| | Transfer the Meringue to a piping bag fitted with a 1/4-inch (.6-cm) star tube and pipe the Meringue over the cakes. |
| | Return to the freezer until ready to serve. |
| | To serve, brown the Meringue with a propane torch adjusted to low flame or in a preheated 500°F (250°C) oven. |
| | Serve immediately with 2 Tbsp (30 mL) of Blueberry Sauce. |

Leah Kalish
Leah's Home
Baking

Leah Kalish has been baking since she uttered her first word, "cookie". Her love for the kitchen was established growing up in a "foodie" family where dinner conversation always included a discussion of the next meal.

She has owned and operated Leah's Home Baking, a pastry catering company, for over 20 years. Leah is best known for her famous biscotti available through caterers and most specialty food shops in Toronto.

# Lemon Meringue Phyllo Nests

## Nests

4 sheets phyllo pastry 4 sheets

¼ cup melted unsalted butter 65 mL

1 Tbsp sugar 30 g

## Lemon Curd

2 lemons 2
   rind finely grated

¼ cup fresh lemon juice 65 mL

½ cup sugar 125 g

2 oz unsalted butter 28 g

5 egg yolks 5

## Meringue Topping

½ cup egg whites 125 mL
   room temperature

¾ cup sugar 150 g

**4 servings**

### Nests

Preheat oven to 350°F (180°C).

Place 1 sheet of phyllo on work surface. Keep remaining sheets covered with a damp cloth.

Brush first sheet lightly with melted butter. Sprinkle with sugar.

Using a dowel or wooden spoon handle, roll phyllo onto dowel and gently press sides together.

Slide off dowel, form a circle with the ends slightly overlapping and pinch the ends together to form a nest. Place on a baking sheet.

Repeat with remaining phyllo sheets.

Bake for approximately 10 minutes or until golden. Cool on wire racks.

### Lemon Curd

In a heavy-bottomed saucepan set over medium heat, stir lemon juice, rind and sugar until dissolved.

Slowly whisk in the eggs. Switch to a wooden spoon, stirring constantly to avoid scrambling the eggs.

Cook until the mixture thickens enough to coat the back of the spoon. Do not allow it to boil.

Remove from the heat and stir in the butter.

Cover with plastic wrap resting on the surface of the curd and refrigerate until ready to use.

| | |
|---|---|
| Meringue Topping | In the bowl of an electric mixer fitted with the whisk attachment, beat the egg whites until stiff. |
| | Very gradually add the sugar in a steady stream. Beat until stiff but not dry. |
| Assembly | Preheat broiler or have propane torch nearby. |
| | Place Nests on a baking sheet. Fill the center of each Nest with Lemon Curd. |
| | Spoon meringue over the curd to cover it completely. |
| | Lightly caramelize the tops using either the broiler or the propane torch set to low flame. |
| | Serve immediately. |

Suzanne Baby
**Gallery Grill at
Hart House**

"Cases of peaches were ordered for the restaurant for an upcoming function. On arrival, they were beautifully ripe, but within a day they began to spoil due to the unusually wet summer.

"In order to save them from disaster, we quickly busied ourselves canning them for future use. About one month later, one of our fridges went on the fritz and froze everything inside. One casualty was an entire case of 35% whipping cream. To prevent any bacteria build-up while defrosting, the cream was brought to a boil then used to make crème fraiche!"

# Preserved Ontario Peaches
## with Crème Fraiche Ice Cream and Macadamia Pralines

### Peaches Canned in Brandy

4-5 ripe freestone peaches 4-5
   blanched, peeled, halved

3-4 cups simple syrup* 750-1000 mL
   steeped with ½ vanilla bean

⅔ cup brandy 160 mL

**\*To make simple syrup**
Mix 2 cups (500 mL) water with 2 ½ cups (600 g) sugar in a medium saucepan. Over medium heat, bring to a boil and stir just to dissolve the sugar. Remove from the heat and cool. Keep in a sealed jar in the fridge.

### Crème Fraiche Ice Cream

1 ½ cups dark brown sugar 330 g

½ cup water 125 mL

8 egg yolks 8

1 cup crème fraiche 250 mL

1 cup 35% whipping cream 250 mL

### Macadamia Praline

¼ cup macadamia nuts 30 g

2 Tbsp + 1 tsp sugar 30 g

**4 servings**

Peaches Canned in Brandy

Sterilize 2 large (1-L) mason jar bottles and lids and dry upside down on a rack.

Divide the peaches among the bottles.

Fill each jar approximately one third full with brandy.

Fill to the top with the vanilla simple syrup.

Screw on the lids and process in boiling water for 20 minutes.

Remove from the water and when cool enough to handle, tighten lids.

Crème Fraiche Ice Cream

Bring brown sugar and water to a boil. Boil until liquid is reduced by half.

In the bowl of an electric mixer fitted with the whisk attachment, beat the egg yolks until thick and pale in color.

Slowly pour in the brown sugar syrup and continue to beat for 1 minute.

Add crème fraiche and 35% whipping cream and mix well.

Chill before freezing in ice cream machine following manufacturer's instructions.

| | |
|---|---|
| Macadamia Praline | Butter a baking tray or line with parchment paper or Silpat. |
| | In a small saucepan with a heavy bottom, heat the nuts with 2 Tbsp (25 g) of the sugar stirring constantly until the sugar melts. |
| | Continue to cook until the sugar caramelizes to a deep golden brown. Pour the mixture onto the prepared pan and sprinkle with enough remaining sugar to coat the top. |
| Assembly | In each of 4 serving bowls, place a scoop of ice cream. |
| | Place a peach half on either side of the ice cream. |
| | Drizzle some of the peach syrup over the ice cream. |
| | Break up the macadamia nut praline into shards and place them into or on top of the ice cream at dramatic angles. |

Suzanne Baby
Gallery Grill at
Hart House

This is an example of the wonderfully creative mind of Suzanne Baby. If you've never eaten at Hart House here's your opportunity to try a new take on traditional pumpkin pie. Warm, cool, crunchy and smooth; elegant and earthy all at the same time. What a terrific dessert!

# Warm Pumpkin Pie
## with Pumpkin Brittle and Frozen Single Malt Mousse

### Frozen Single Malt Mousse

½ cup sugar 100 g

⅜ cup water 95 mL

4 egg yolks 4

1-2 oz malt whisky 28-56 mL
  to taste

1 cup 35% whipping cream 250 mL

### Pumpkin Seed Brittle

½ cup toasted pumpkin seeds 75 g
  (in their shells)

1 cup sugar 200 g

¼ cup water 65 mL

### Pastry Shells

4 cups all-purpose flour 560 g

⅔ cup sugar 130 g

1 tsp baking powder 5 mL

½ tsp salt 2 mL

2 sticks unsalted butter 227 g
  cubed

4 eggs 4
  beaten

15 oz can pumpkin pie filling 420 mL

1 bunch fresh mint sprigs 1 bunch

icing sugar

6 servings

### Frozen Single Malt Mousse

Line six 1/2 cup (125 mL) ramekins, coffee cups or Jell-O molds with plastic wrap. Set aside.

In a small, heavy-bottomed saucepan, cook sugar and water to soft ball stage (230°F/121°C).

Meanwhile, in the bowl of an electric mixer fitted with the whisk attachment, whip the yolks until very thick and pale in color.

When the sugar syrup has arrived at the proper temperature, slowly pour it into the eggs with the machine running, being careful not to pour it onto the whisk.

Add the whisky and continue to whip the eggs until they are cool.

In a chilled bowl, with a chilled whisk, whip the whipping cream into very soft peaks.

Using a hand whisk, fold the cream into the egg yolks.

Pour the batter into the prepared molds and freeze until firm.

When ready to assemble the entire dessert, unmold onto a tray, cover with plastic wrap and replace in the freezer.

### Pumpkin Seed Brittle

Oil a flat baking sheet or line with parchment paper or Silpat.

Spread the seeds evenly over two thirds of the sheet.

In a small, heavy-bottomed saucepan, cook sugar and water until it turns a light caramel color.

Pour the liquid over the seeds and allow it to harden.

Cut half the brittle into small pieces. Crush the rest to a medium grain powder.

| | |
|---|---|
| Pastry Shells | Preheat the oven to 350°F (180°C). |

Put the dry ingredients into the bowl of a food processor fitted with the steel blade and process to mix, about 5 seconds.

Add the butter cubes and pulse only enough to make a coarse meal consistency.

Add the eggs and pulse until just mixed. Don't overmix!

Remove and divide in half, patting dough into round discs. Wrap and refrigerate for about 2 hours.

Roll out the dough to 1/8 inch (.3 cm) thickness. Use a 6-inch (15-cm) round cookie cutter to cut rounds of dough to be fitted into six 4-inch (10-cm) tart shell pans. Trim the edges flush with the rims of the pans.

Place the pans on a cookie sheet and bake in the oven 10-12 minutes or until pastry begins to turn a light golden brown.

Cool.

**To assemble the tarts**

Preheat oven to 375°F (190°C).

Fill the tart shells with pumpkin filling.

Bake for 5-10 minutes or until heated through.

Place on a round plate and top with 1 frozen whisky mousse.

Scatter brittle pieces over top. Dust the entire plate with brittle powder and icing sugar. Garnish with a sprig of mint.

Dufflet Rosenberg
Dufflet Pastries

"As simple as it is, this elegant raspberry tart exemplifies what perfect pastry-making is all about: balance and contrast. The assertive, acidic flavor of raspberries plays perfectly against mellow vanilla custard and buttery, sweet, yet crisp pastry.

My secret is to use both sour cream and whipping cream for the custard and the best vanilla possible (from Tahiti or Madagascar). The tart is wonderful finished brûléed (as in crème brûlée) or could simply be topped with more fresh raspberries."

# Raspberry Tarts

## Sweet Pastry for Tart Shells

1 ¾ cups all-purpose flour 245 g

½ cup cake and pastry flour 70 g

½ cup + 2 Tbsp sugar 125 g

pinch salt pinch

1 cup unsalted butter 227 g
    cut into ½-inch (1.2-cm) pieces

2 egg yolks 2

¼ cup 35% whipping cream 65 mL

## Filling

¾ cup icing sugar 90 g

2 eggs 2

½ cup 35% whipping cream 125 mL

½ cup sour cream 125 mL

1 tsp vanilla 5 mL

¼ cup turbinado sugar 40 g

1 ½ cups fresh raspberries 210 g
    (about 2 pints)

**10 tarts**

### Sweet Pastry for Tart Shells

Place the flours, sugar, and salt in the bowl of an electric mixer fitted with the paddle attachment. Add the butter.

On low speed, break up the butter into the flour until mixture resembles oat flakes.

Blend the egg yolks with the whipping cream. Slowly add to the flour/butter mixture mixing on low speed. Mix only until just combined.

Remove and pat into a flat disc. Wrap in plastic and chill for 1 hour.

Preheat oven to 375°F (190°C).

Remove dough from the fridge and divide evenly into 10 pieces.

Form each piece into a disc. On a lightly floured surface, roll dough pieces into circles large enough to fit into a 3 1/2-inch (8.7-cm) straight-sided tart pan. The dough circle will be 4 1/2 –5 inches (11.2–12.5 cm) in diameter.

Press the dough into the pans, being sure that the sides are snug with the bottom and that any air pockets are removed. Trim the edges.

Place on 2 baking sheets and refrigerate until dough is once again firm, 20-30 minutes.

Remove from the fridge and prick with a fork. Line each tart with foil and fill with beans or pie weights.

Bake for 10 minutes and remove the foil and beans, continuing to bake until light golden brown.

Set aside to cool.

Filling

Turn oven down to 325°F (160°C).

Combine the icing sugar, eggs, cream, sour cream, and vanilla. Whisk until smooth.

Divide the berries evenly among the prepared tart shells, about 6 per shell.

Pour or ladle the cream filling evenly over the berries.

Bake until the crust is golden brown and the filling is set, 25-30 minutes.

Let tarts cool before removing from pans. Chill.

Sprinkle each tart with some of the turbinado sugar. Use a propane torch set on a low flame to caramelize the sugar. Or, place the tarts on a cookie sheet and place them under the broiler, watching them so that they don't burn.

Esther Benaim &
Maggie McKeown
**Great Cooks &
The T Spot**

"Maggie and I love pears poached this way. For some reason, we find them sexy. Along with our Chicken Tagine (p 142) these were featured recently on *Christine Cushing Live*. We think you'll find them deliciously different. You can purchase mandarin chai tea directly from us or you can substitute any tea."

# Chai Poached Pears Stuffed
## with Ginger Mascarpone Served with a Mandarin Chai Sauce

8 cups boiling water 2 L

4 tsp mandarin chai tea 20 mL

1 cup sugar 200 g

4 pears 4
    just ripe, peeled, halved and cored

1 cup mascarpone cheese 250 mL

¼ cup candied ginger 30 g
    finely chopped

1 tsp vanilla 5 mL

1 orange 1
    rind finely grated

¼ cup 35% whipping cream 65 mL

¼ cup honey 65 mL

cinnamon as garnish

4 sprigs fresh mint 4 sprigs

**4 servings**

In a 10-quart (10-L) pot, pour the boiling water over the tea and let infuse for 3-5 minutes according to preference.

Add the sugar, bring to a boil and reduce the heat. Stir to dissolve the sugar.

Add the pear halves and simmer for 15-20 minutes or until fork tender.

Remove the pears and place in a low-sided pan with just enough poaching liquid to keep them moist.

Mix the mascarpone with the candied ginger and vanilla until smooth.

Add 2 Tbsp of the pear poaching liquid, or just enough to make the mixture loose enough to pipe but still thick enough to hold its shape when piped. It should be thick and creamy, like whipped cream.

Place the mascarpone into a piping bag fitted with a 1/2-inch (1.2-cm) plain piping tube.

Pipe two dabs of mascarpone cheese on each of 4 plates. The cheese will anchor the pears in place.

Place 2 pear halves on each plate, anchoring the bottom larger half on the dab of mascarpone.

Pipe or mound the mascarpone in the center of each pear half.

Place 1 cup (250 mL) of the pear poaching liquid and the orange rind in a small saucepan. Bring to a boil.

In a second small saucepan, mix together the cream and the honey. Bring to a boil.

Add to the simmering pear poaching liquid and stir to blend.

Spoon the sauce around the base of the pears. Lightly sift cinnamon over each plate and garnish with mint sprig.

Joanne Yolles

Freelance Pastry
Chef

"During my days (and nights) at Scaramouche, this dessert
was wildly popular. Who would have thought it?"

# Rhubarb Berry Crisp

### Filling

4 cups fresh rhubarb 1 L
  cut into ½-inch (1.2-cm) pieces,
  approximately 2-3 bundles

4 cups fresh raspberries, blackberries
  and/or strawberries 1 L
  cut into halves or quarters

1 cup sugar 250 mL
  or to taste

⅓ cup cornstarch 30 g

1 Tbsp fresh lemon juice 15 g


### Topping

½ cup sugar 100 g

¼ cup + 1Tbsp brown sugar 70 g

½ cup toasted wheat germ 55 g

½ cup all-purpose flour 60 g

½ tsp cinnamon 2 mL

½ tsp nutmeg 2 mL

⅔ cup unsalted butter 150 g
  cubed room temperature

1 cup rolled oats 100 g

¾ cup slivered almonds or pecans 90 g


### 8 servings

Preheat oven to 350°F (180°C).

Combine all the fruit filling ingredients in a bowl and
let stand 10 minutes.

For the topping, combine the sugar, brown sugar, wheat
germ, flour, cinnamon, and nutmeg in a bowl.

Add the butter and crumble with your fingertips. Once
the butter is incorporated add the rolled oats and nuts
and toss gently to combine.

Place the fruit in a 3-quart (3-L) baking dish and top
with the crumble mixture.

Bake until the top is golden and the fruit is bubbling,
about 50 minutes. Serve warm with Crème Anglaise.
(See Crème Anglaise recipe pp 19-20.)

Wanda Beaver

Wanda's Pie
in the Sky

"I love pumpkin pie, but if I had to choose, I would take this pie in a minute. Its creamy, spicy filling is similar to pumpkin but the combination of crunchy pecan crust, maple nut praline and maple syrup drizzle elevates it to another level.

"We featured this pie at Eat to the Beat 1999. I personally served it to hundreds of guests, and even though I had to twist a few arms in order for some people to sample it (we're talking about vegetable and dessert in one breath, after all!), the response was overwhelming: it was a runaway hit."

# Sweet Potato Praline Pie

### Crust

1 ¼ cup pecans 150 g

1 ¼ cup all-purpose flour 175 g

⅔ cup sugar 130 g

⅓ cup unsalted butter 75 g
  chilled, cubed

2 Tbsp water 30 mL

### Filling

5 eggs 5

1 cup brown sugar 220 g

2 tsp cinnamon 10 mL

¼ tsp salt 1 mL

2 ½ cups sweet potatoes 540 mL
  cooked, mashed

¾ cup 35% whipping cream 185 mL

1 ½ cups milk 375 mL

1 tsp vanilla 5 mL

Preheat oven to 350°F (180°C).

Crust

In the bowl of a food processor fitted with the steel blade, place the pecans, flour, sugar and butter and process until they resemble coarse meal and just begin to clump.

Add the water and process only until dough starts to come together.

Remove; press into a 10-inch x 1 1/4-inch (25-cm x 3.2-cm) flan pan with a removable bottom.

Bake for 20 minutes or until set and a light golden brown. Set aside to cool.

Filling

In the bowl of an electric mixer fitted with the whisk attachment, beat together the eggs, brown sugar, cinnamon and salt until light and foamy.

Add the sweet potato, cream, milk, and vanilla and beat until smooth.

Pour into the pre-baked crust.

Bake for 35-45 minutes until just set. Cool.

Reduce the oven to 325°F (160°C).

## Praline

$\frac{1}{3}$ cup brown sugar 75 g

$\frac{1}{2}$ cup maple syrup 125 mL

2 Tbsp unsalted butter 30 g

2 cups pecan halves 240 g

## Topping

1 cup 35% whipping cream 250 mL

$\frac{1}{2}$ tsp vanilla 2 mL

1 Tbsp sugar 12 g

$\frac{1}{2}$ cup maple syrup 125 mL

**10 servings**

## Praline

Butter a baking sheet and line it with parchment paper or Silpat. Butter a second baking sheet but do not line. Set both aside.

In a heavy-bottomed, medium saucepan combine the brown sugar, maple syrup and butter.

Cook over medium heat, stirring constantly until the sugar is dissolved and the mixture is boiling. Boil for 2-3 minutes.

Add the pecans and stir to coat them completely in the caramel.

Spread the coated pecans on the buttered baking sheet in a single layer.

Bake for 15-20 minutes, turning occasionally until dark golden brown.

Remove from the oven and spread on unlined baking sheet, separating the pecans. Cool.

For topping, whip cream with sugar and vanilla.

## Assembly

Place a wedge of pie on each plate. Mound some whipped cream on the side of the pie. Sprinkle with pralines and drizzle plate with maple syrup.

Sandy Kaminker
Freelance Pastry
Chef / Caterer

# Lemon Fruit Trifle

## Simple Syrup

¼ cup water 65 mL

¼ cup sugar 50 g

¼ cup orange liqueur 65 mL

## Strawberry Sauce

2 pints fresh strawberries 340-400 g
   hulled, washed

¼ cup sugar 50 g

2 tsp fresh lemon juice 10 mL

## Lemon Curd Filling

6 eggs 6
   room temperature

4 egg yolks 4

2 ½ cups sugar 500 g

2 lemons 2
   rind finely grated

1 cup less 1 Tbsp lemon juice 235 mL

½ cup melted unsalted butter 112 g

### Simple Syrup

Combine water and sugar in a small saucepan.

On medium heat, stir sugar with a wooden spoon only until it is dissolved.

Bring syrup to a boil over medium high heat and boil for 3 minutes.

Transfer to a small bowl and stir in liqueur.

Cool. When cold, refrigerate tightly covered.

### Strawberry Sauce

Purée the berries in a food processor.

Strain purée through a fine sieve into a large, microwaveable bowl.

Stir in sugar and lemon juice.

Microwave, uncovered, on high for 15-20 minutes. Reduce the purée until it achieves the consistency of a thickened heavy cream.

Editor's Note
While you can reduce the purée on the stove, using the microwave reduces the risk of caramelizing the sugar and therefore losing the strong strawberry flavor.

### Lemon Curd Filling

In a heavy-bottomed saucepan over medium heat, beat the eggs and the yolks together.

Add the sugar gradually and whisk lightly to combine.

Add the lemon rind and juice and whisk to blend.

Add the melted butter.

Use a wooden spoon to stir constantly over medium heat until mixture is as thick as heavy cream and can coat the back of the spoon, approximately 15 minutes. Do not boil.

1 genoise or cake layer 1
   10-inch diameter (25 cm)
   may be store-bought or homemade

1 cup blackberry or raspberry jam
   250 mL

1 ripe mango 1

1 pint each raspberries and blueberries
   170 g

1 cup 35% whipping cream 250 mL

1 cup assorted berries 170 g
   for finishing

icing sugar


**8-10 servings**


Place a strainer over a medium bowl and pour the curd through it.

Let cool. Curd will firm up as it cools down.

Once it has cooled, set a piece of plastic wrap directly on the surface of the curd to prevent a skin from forming. Refrigerate until ready to use.


Assembly

Have ready a clear glass bowl with a 10-inch (25-cm) diameter.

Slice cake layer horizontally into 3 layers.

Pour approximately 1/4 cup (50 mL) Strawberry Sauce into the bowl and to cover the bottom.

Place 1 cake layer over the Strawberry Sauce.

Brush the cake layer liberally with Simple Syrup.

Spread a thin layer of blackberry jam over the cake.

Top with a handful of mixed berries and mango pieces.

Dribble some Strawberry Sauce over the fruit.

Top with one-third of the Lemon Curd.

Repeat the layering process 2 more times ending with Lemon Curd.

At this point, the cake may be covered with plastic wrap and refrigerated for up to 2 days prior to serving.

When ready to serve, whip the cream to soft peak stage.

Spread cream on top of the trifle and arrange mixed berries on top.

Right before serving, sift a light layer of icing sugar over the top.

Anne Yarymowich

**The Agora at the
Art Gallery of Ontario**

"The AGO's proximity to Chinatown puts us in touch with the seasonality of many exotic ingredients. In November and December, when persimmons start to appear on the street stands in Chinatown, we like to prepare this wonderful and surprisingly comforting dessert, which was adapted from a recipe in *Saveur* magazine. Persimmons when prepared this way remind me of dates, in flavor and texture. Either of the two varieties of persimmons is suitable for this recipe, as long as they are very ripe, meaning soft and yielding to the touch and a dark, burnt-orange in color."

# Persimmon Pudding

2 cups very ripe persimmon pulp
   500 mL about 8-10 persimmons

1 tsp baking soda 5 mL

1 ½ cups buttermilk 375 mL

2 cups sugar 400 g

2 eggs 2

1 ½ cups all-purpose flour 210 g

1 tsp baking powder 5 mL

½ tsp cardamom 2 mL

½ tsp cinnamon 2 mL

pinch salt pinch

¼ cup melted unsalted butter 65 mL

¼ cup whipped cream 65 mL
   or Crème Anglaise (pp 19-20)

**12 servings**

Preheat oven to 350°F (180°C). Lightly grease the sides and bottom of twelve 4-oz (125-mL) ramekins with vegetable spray. Line the bottoms with parchment paper. Tie 3-inch (7.5-cm) parchment paper collars around the outside of each ramekin. Set aside.

Purée the persimmon pulp and pass through a fine sieve.

In a medium bowl stir baking soda into buttermilk. Set aside.

In the bowl of an electric mixer fitted with the paddle attachment, mix together pulp and sugar.

Add the eggs and beat until smooth on low speed.

Add buttermilk mixture and mix until blended.

In a separate bowl, mix dry ingredients together and toss with a fork.

Gradually add dry ingredients to the mixture in the mixing bowl and mix only until moistened.

Add the whipped cream and the melted butter.

Fill to 1/2 inch (1.2 cm) from the top of the ramekin (they will rise high as they bake and fall as they cool.)

Bake for 50-60 minutes.

Let cool and remove gently from the ramekin by inverting onto a plate.

Serve at room temperature accompanied by whipped cream or Crème Anglaise.

Leah Kalish
Leah's Home
Baking

Although associated with Australia, the Pavlova actually originated in New Zealand. It is a wonderful combination of things soft and crunchy, sweet and cool, fresh and baked. It is also a great solution to the Passover dilemma of something new and different. Just don't try it on a humid day!

# Pavlova

2 cups egg whites 500 mL
   room temperature

2¾ cups sugar 550 g

2 cups 35% whipping cream 500 mL

¼ cup sugar 50 g

1 tsp vanilla 5 mL

½ pint blackberries 100 g

½ pint raspberries 100 g

1 pint blueberries 170 g

1 pint strawberries 170 g
   quartered with stems removed

8 servings

Preheat oven to 225°F (115°C). Trace 2 large ovals, about 12 inches (30 cm) long, on parchment paper. Turn them over and place on 2 baking pans.

In the bowl of an electric mixer fitted with the whisk attachment, beat the egg whites to the stiff but not dry stage.

Very gradually, add sugar in a slow stream, beating until very stiff peaks are formed.

With a plain piping tip, or a big spoon, form an oval following the traced outline. Create a 2-inch (5-cm) border surrounding the center of the oval by piping or spooning more meringue around the sides than in the center.

Bake for 4 hours or leave in the oven overnight at 175°F (85°C). Cool.

When ready to serve, whip cream to soft peak stage and gradually beat in the sugar. Beat on medium speed for 1 or 2 minutes more and add vanilla. Mix only to blend.

Spoon whipped cream inside meringues in billowy mounds. Top with berries and serve immediately.

Anna Olson
On the Twenty

"This dessert also makes a delicious breakfast! I like to cook this at home because I can prepare it at the last minute and use whatever fruit I have handy. The fruit combination I have used below highlights autumn or winter flavors, but certainly summer's finest pick of peaches, apricots, and cherries would make a delicious variation. 'Skyr' is the Scandinavian version of yogurt cheese and must be prepared a day ahead."

# Sweet Honey Polenta
## with Skyr and Fruit Compote

### Skyr

3 cups plain, full fat yogurt 750 mL
3 Tbsp sugar 40 g

### Polenta

3 cups milk 750 mL
½ cup cornmeal 60 g
½ cup less 1 Tbsp honey 100 mL
2 tsp vanilla 10 mL
¼ cup 35% whipping cream 65 mL

### Poached Fruits

1 pear 200 g
   peeled, cored, diced
1 apple 200 g
   peeled, cored, diced
¼ cup dried apricots 45 g
¼ cup dried prunes 45 g
¼ cup dried cherries 40 g
½ cup white wine 125 mL
½ cup sugar 100 g
1 Tbsp vanilla 15 mL
2 Earl Grey tea bags 2

**6 servings**

### Skyr

Set a strainer lined with a clean dishtowel or cheese-cloth over a bowl. Spoon yogurt into the strainer.

Place in the refrigerator overnight. The whey will separate from the milk solids in the strainer.

Scrape off the rich and thickened Skyr and stir in the sugar.

### Sweet Polenta

For polenta, heat milk in a medium saucepan over medium heat until just below a simmer.

Whisk in cornmeal gradually. Cook over medium heat, stirring constantly, until milk has been absorbed and polenta is tender, about 15 minutes.

Add honey, vanilla and whipping cream and stir in well.

Serve warm, but note that polenta will thicken as it sits.

### Poached Fruits

Place all the ingredients in a medium saucepan set over medium heat and bring to a simmer, stirring regularly until fresh fruits are tender and dried fruits are plump, 15-20 minutes. Remove tea bags.

To serve, ladle the polenta into bowls, top with the warm fruit and a dollop of Skyr.

Lynn Mendelson
Caterer

"This recipe originally called for two egg yolks. I found the recipe was perfect … but only if I nibbled away quite significantly at the batter while I was spreading it. I found that when I was dieting, which is most of the time, the bottom layer is too much like a cookie and not enough like toffee. So I discovered that when you reduce the egg yolk to one, the base is perfect for me … even when I'm on a diet!!!"

# Almond Rococo Bars

1 cup sugar 200 g

1 cup brown sugar 220 g

¾ lb unsalted butter 340 g
   softened

1 tsp vanilla 5 mL

dash salt dash

1 egg yolk 1

2 cups all-purpose flour 280 g

10 oz milk chocolate 280 g melted

¾ cups toasted almonds 90 g
   slivered

32 bars

Preheat oven to 350°F (180°C).

Grease 12-inch x 16-inch (30-cm x 40-cm) jelly roll pan with vegetable spray or line with parchment paper.

In the bowl of a food processor, process sugar and brown sugar to blend.

Add butter and process until fluffy.

Add vanilla, salt and egg yolk. Process to blend.

Add flour and process until the mixture comes away from the pan.

Pat or spread the batter in the prepared pan. If sticky, dust your palms lightly with flour.

Bake for 40-45 minutes.

Remove from the oven and cover with melted milk chocolate.

Sprinkle with toasted almonds.

Cool for about 20 minutes before cutting into squares.

Dufflet Rosenberg
**Dufflet Pastries**

"I'm constantly asked, 'What's your favorite dessert?' Meringues! It all started in France where, as a teen, I discovered how wonderful crunchy meringue layered with smooth buttercream could be. No one was making a classic *dacquoise* in Toronto, so I created my own version of my favorite, Cappuccino Dacquoise. Today the Cappuccino Dacquoise is a signature Dufflet cake."

# Bite-Size Cappuccino Hazelnut Dacquoise

## Hazelnut Meringue Layers

6 Tbsp icing sugar 45 g unsifted

½ cup toasted hazelnuts 56 g coarsely ground

2 egg whites 2

3 Tbsp sugar 40 g

## Coffee Buttercream

6 egg yolks 6

¾ cup sugar 150 g

½ cup corn syrup 125 mL

2 cups unsalted butter 454 g softened

2 Tbsp instant coffee 30 mL dissolved in 2 Tbsp (30 mL) water

3 Tbsp cocoa powder 25 g

24 chocolate-covered coffee beans 24

**12 servings**

### Hazelnut Meringue Layers

Preheat oven to 200°F (95°C).

Line 2 baking pans with parchment paper. If desired, trace twenty-four 1 1/2-inch (3.7-cm)–1 3/4-inch (4.2-cm) circles on each piece of parchment paper as a piping guide. Flip the paper over so you pipe on the unmarked side.

In small bowl, combine icing sugar and hazelnuts and set aside.

Place the egg whites in the mixing bowl of an electric mixer fitted with the whisk attachment. On medium speed, beat the egg whites until frothy.

Gradually, add 1 Tbsp (14 g) sugar. Continue to beat another minute to the soft peak stage and gradually add the remaining 2 Tbsp (28 g) sugar. Continue to beat 1 more minute or until stiff peaks are formed.

Remove the bowl from the mixer and using a balloon whisk or a rubber spatula, gently but thoroughly fold in the nut/sugar mixture.

Fit a piping bag with a #12 plain decorator's tip. Fill the piping bag with the meringue and pipe discs onto the parchment, starting at the center and working out in concentric circles.

Bake for about 2 hours or until the discs are very dry and crisp.

Store in airtight container if not assembling immediately.

### Coffee Buttercream

Place the egg yolks in the mixing bowl of an electric mixer fitted with the whisk attachment. Beat until light in color.

## Coffee Buttercream

**Note**
This recipe makes twice as much as is needed for this recipe. Store any unused buttercream in an air-tight container and freeze.

Combine the sugar and corn syrup in a small saucepan. Over medium high heat, bring ingredients to a rolling boil, stirring constantly.

Transfer to a glass measuring cup with a pouring spout.

Turn the mixer to low speed and add one-quarter to one-third of the sugar syrup to the egg yolks.

Increase the speed and continue beating to incorporate the syrup. Add the syrup in 2 or 3 more additions, slowing the speed to add and increasing it to incorporate after each addition.

Continue to beat until the mixture is completely cool.

On medium speed, gradually incorporate the softened butter, about 1 Tbsp (15 mL) at a time. Add the coffee mixture and mix until incorporated.

## Assembly

Place 24 of the discs on a baking sheet.

Fit a piping bag with 1/4-inch (.6 cm) star tip and fill with buttercream.

Starting at the outside edge, pipe buttercream in a concentric circle to cover the disc.

Top with another meringue disc, piped side up.

Fill a small sieve or tea strainer with the cocoa. Hold it over the dacquoise. Using the tip of a paring knife gently tap the edge of the strainer so that a fine, even coating of cocoa falls on top of the pastry.

Place 1 chocolate coffee bean in the center of each dacquoise.

Refrigerate for at least 2 hours before serving. Can be made one day in advance. May be frozen, well-wrapped, before sifted with cocoa, for about 1 month.

Ayoma Fonseka

**Ayoma Cake
Masterpieces**

Everyone loves a sweet. And Ayoma's are usually spectacular wedding cakes, which take hours in the making. But she is also a master chocolatier and has supplied us with two great, easy recipes guaranteed to impress. Here's the first one. The other is on page 84.

# Coconut Munchies

½ cup 35% whipping cream 125 mL

1 Tbsp unsalted butter 14 g

12 oz bittersweet chocolate 335 g
  chopped

1 ½ tsp vanilla 7 mL

10 oz package unsweetened coconut
  280 g

2 cups cashew nuts 227 g

**32 pieces**

Line a baking pan with parchment paper or arrange with paper or foil bonbon cups. Have a teaspoon ready.

In a heavy saucepan, boil cream and butter.

Remove from heat and add chopped chocolate and stir until smooth.

Add vanilla and mix.

Add coconut and cashew nuts.

Use teaspoon to drop small mounds of batter directly on to the pan or into the bonbon cups.

Chill until firm.

Lisa Slater

Co-Founder
Eat to the Beat /
Whole Foods
Market

"My grandfather owned restaurants and a large coffee business in New York City. My dad worked in both businesses and his enthusiasm for the business side as well as my mother's love of the food and design side made it easy for me to turn into a restaurateur.

"My first restaurant was in New York City. Eventually I moved to Toronto and opened a series of businesses with my sister Abigail. Together, we ran bakeries, restaurants, prepared food and gourmet stores and finally, 12 bagel stores."

# Peanut Butter-White Chocolate Swirl Cheesecake
## with Blood Orange Sauce

### Crust

1 box chocolate wafer cookies 1 box

3 Tbsp good quality peanuts 60 g

¼ cup melted butter 65 mL

### Filling

2 8-oz packages cream cheese 454 g

2 large eggs 2

¾ cup sugar 150 g

¼ cup white chocolate 65 mL
    melted

⅔ cup peanut butter 150 g
    chunky or smooth

¼ cup bittersweet chocolate 65 mL
    melted

1 vanilla bean 1
    split

**10 servings**

### Crust

Preheat oven to 350°F (180°C).

In the bowl of a food processor fitted with the steel blade, place the cookies and peanuts. Process until fine crumbs are formed.

Add butter and process briefly to coat the crumbs.

Press the crumbs into a 10-inch (25-cm) springform pan lined with a round of parchment paper.

Bake for 8 minutes and cool on a wire rack. Wrap the bottom of the pan with aluminum foil, about 2 inches (5 cm) up the sides.

Reduce oven temperature to 300°F (150°C).

### Filling

Have a shallow roasting pan and boiling water to fill it half-way at hand.

Place the cream cheese, eggs and sugar in the bowl of a food processor fitted with the steel blade. Process until smooth.

Scrape the seeds of the vanilla bean into the mixture and process to blend thoroughly. Scrape the sides as required.

Add the white chocolate and process to blend completely.

Pour 1 cup (250 mL) of batter into each of 2 small bowls.

Add the peanut butter to one and the melted dark chocolate to the other. Whisk to blend each mixture thoroughly.

continued

# Peanut Butter-White Chocolate Swirl Cheesecake (continued)

## Glaze

1 cup + 2 Tbsp 35% whipping cream
  280 mL

5 oz bittersweet chocolate 140 g
  chopped

4 oz white chocolate 112 g
  chopped

1 Tbsp peanuts 15 mL
  coarsely chopped

white chocolate curls

## Blood Orange Sauce

1 cup blood orange juice 250 mL

¼ cup or to taste sugar 50 g or to taste

pinch salt pinch

2 tsp cornstarch 10 mL
  dissolved in 1 Tbsp (15 mL)
  cold water

1 Tbsp orange liqueur 15 mL
  (optional)


garnish fresh mint slivers

Pour the remaining plain batter into the prepared shell and smooth with an offset spatula.

First, drizzle the peanut butter batter in a thin stream over the batter in the pan to create a marbleized effect. Let it sit for a minute so that it can settle into the batter.

Next, drizzle the chocolate batter over the first 2 batters to enhance the marbleized effect.

Run the tip of a knife in a zig-zag pattern through all three batters, being careful not to touch the bottom crust. Do this once or twice to mingle the batters.

Place the pan in the roasting pan and place in the oven.

Pour enough boiling water to come halfway up the aluminum foil, and bake for 30-40 minutes or until the cake is set but still wobbly in the center.

Turn off the oven and open the door. Allow pan to sit in the oven for half an hour.

Remove pan from the oven and cool to room temperature on a wire rack.

When completely cool, cover with plastic wrap and chill thoroughly.


Glazes

Place whipping cream in a small saucepan and bring barely to a boil.

Place chopped chocolates in 2 separate bowls. Pour hot cream evenly over 2 chocolates. Let sit for 5 minutes.

Whisk each chocolate with a clean whisk.

Pour dark chocolate all at once into the center of the cheesecake.

Lift the pan and rotate so that glaze covers entire surface.

Sprinkle evenly with chopped peanuts.

Use a fork to drizzle the white chocolate glaze over the top of the cake, or, alternatively, shave white chocolate curls all over the top.

Chill until glaze is set.

To remove cake from pan, first wrap a towel soaked in hot water around the edges to melt the chocolate glaze. Then run the tip of a knife, dipped in hot water and dried, around the outside edge of the cake.

Remove the springform ring.

Slip a wide, long spatula under the parchment paper and gently lift the cake.

Slide it onto a serving platter.

**Blood Orange Sauce**

Place orange juice in a small saucepan and add sugar.

Over medium heat cook to dissolve sugar, stirring occasionally.

Add pinch of salt. Stir to dissolve.

Add cornstarch and start stirring with a whisk.

Whisk until sauce has thickened and is clear and shiny.

Strain sauce through a sieve and add the optional orange liqueur.

**To Serve**

Use a knife dipped in hot water and wiped clean after every slice to make perfect slices.

Pool some Blood Orange Sauce on the plate and set the slice in the center.

Garnish with slivers of fresh mint strewn on the sauce.

Izabela Kalabis
Inniskillin Wine

"The love of nuts appears to be genetic in my family. When I was a child in Poland, all special occasions were celebrated with some sort of nut-based cake. Everyone in my family owns this recipe, dating back to old Polish cookbooks, and it has adorned the table of many family get-togethers. Black walnuts have a particular and wonderful taste. They are, however, quite difficult to find, in which case regular walnuts may be substituted."

# Black Walnut Cake

10 egg yolks 10

2 ¼ cups sugar 250 g

2 vanilla beans 2
  split

1 Tbsp bittersweet chocolate 15 mL
  melted

1 cup black walnuts 250 g
  ground*

10 egg whites 10

2 cups icing sugar 250 g
  sifted

3 Tbsp bread/cookie crumbs 50 g

1 cup ground almonds 250 g

1 Tbsp lemon juice 15 mL

icing sugar

**8-10 servings**

*Black walnuts do, indeed, grow in Canada. According to an Internet chef friend, they grow in the Ottawa region but you have to know how to identify them. Frequently, farmers at local markets can tell you where to find them in your area. Their flavor is so distinct, they are worth finding close to home although you can buy them packaged in some US grocery stores, especially those in the South, and freeze them for future use.

Preheat oven to 350°F (180°C). Grease a 9-inch (23-cm) cake pan and line the bottom with parchment paper.

In the bowl of an electric mixer fitted with the whisk attachment, beat the egg yolks and sugar until thick and light.

Scrape the seeds out of 1 vanilla bean into the eggs. Fold in gently.

Fold in the melted chocolate and the walnuts until just combined.

Pour into prepared cake pan and spread evenly.

Wash the whisk and proceed with the egg whites.

In the bowl of an electric mixer fitted with the whisk attachment, beat egg whites until soft peak stage. Gradually add icing sugar and continue beating until stiff but not dry.

Remove from the mixer and gently but thoroughly fold in the bread/cookie crumbs, almonds, scraped vanilla seeds from the second bean and lemon juice.

Pour the egg white batter on top of the black walnut batter already in the pan. Spread evenly.

Bake for 55 minutes or until a skewer tests clean.

Let cool on a wire rack for about 30 minutes before removing from the pan.

Dust lightly with icing sugar before serving.

Bridget Lunn

Private Caterer

"The course of my affair with good food was tortuous, the seed germinating through a frustrating sojourn in Canadian theatre, a chef's journeyman-ship via George Brown College, to stints at the Park Plaza and King Edward hotels, sous-chef at David Wood Catering, private chef in Princeton, N.J. to Hollinger Inc. where today I happily (wo)man the kitchen of the corporate boardroom. Biscotti are among my favorite cookies. These biscotti, as well as the Walnut-Black Pepper Biscotti (see p 66), were served at Eat to the Beat and show off the versatility of two favorite spices."

# Triple Ginger Biscotti

½ cup butter 112 g

1 cup sugar 200 g

2 eggs 2

¾ tsp almond extract 3 mL

2 Tbsp fresh ginger 10 g
    peeled and grated

1 tsp baking powder 5 mL

½ tsp baking soda 2 mL

pinch salt pinch

2 cups unbleached, all-purpose flour
    280 g

2 tsp ground ginger 10 mL

½ tsp cinnamon 2 mL

1 cup whole almonds 120 g

¾ cup candied ginger 100 g
    coarsely chopped

**36 cookies**

Preheat oven to 350°F (180°C).

Cover a cookie tray with parchment paper. Set aside.

In the bowl of an electric mixer fitted with the paddle attachment, beat the butter and sugar until fluffy.

Add the eggs 1 at a time until well blended. Scrape the sides of the bowl after each addition.

Add the almond extract, ginger, baking powder, baking soda and salt. Blend well.

Mix ground ginger and cinnamon with flour. Add to butter mixture, mixing only until completely blended.

Remove bowl from the machine and fold in almonds and candied ginger by hand.

Dip your hands in some flour and divide the dough in half.

Form each half into a flat log, about 12 inches (30 cm) long and 3 inches (2.5 cm) wide.

Sprinkle with sugar.

Bake 20-25 minutes until light brown.

Cool out of the oven for 10 minutes.

With a serrated knife, slice the loaf into 1-inch (2.5-cm) slices.

Place cut side down on baking sheet.

Return to the oven and bake an additional 15 minutes until golden brown and crisp.

Cool. Store in an airtight tin.

Wanda Beaver

Wanda's Pie
in the Sky

"There is no known cure! One bite of these and you'll forget about chocolate! Once, when we participated in a food festival, we sold out the entire weekend's allotment the first day so I was back in the bakery until late that night baking some more. The next day, we even raised the price in hopes of slowing down the frenzied consumption of our treat, but to no avail! So … you have been warned! There is no known cure!"

# Butterscotch Brownies

### Batter

2 ½ cups dark brown sugar 550 g

3 eggs 3

2 tsp vanilla 10 mL

1 cup unsalted butter 227 mL
     melted

1 Tbsp baking powder 15 g

1 ½ cup all-purpose flour 210 g

½ tsp salt 2 mL

2 cups walnuts or pecans 200 g

### Butterscotch Topping

1 ½ cups brown sugar 330 g

½ cup water 125 mL

½ cup 35% whipping cream 125 mL

½ cup unsalted butter 55 g

1 tsp vanilla 5 mL

1 cup walnuts or pecans 200 g
     chopped

### 24 servings

Preheat oven to 325°F (160°C).

Grease a 9-inch x 13-inch (23-cm x 33-cm) baking pan and line with foil overhanging the ends of the pan. Grease bottom and sides again.

In the bowl of an electric mixer fitted with the beater attachment, cream together the brown sugar, eggs and vanilla.

Add melted butter and mix thoroughly.

Mix together the flour, baking powder and salt. Set aside.

Add dry ingredients to the batter and mix well.

Add nuts and blend to incorporate.

Spread batter evenly in the pan.

Bake 40-45 minutes until puffed in the center and golden brown all around. Do not overbake!

Cool in the pan. Lift the brownie slab out of the pan and peel off the foil. Allow to cool.

Topping

In a heavy-bottomed saucepan, bring the sugar and water to a boil. As the sugar begins to turn a light brown and caramelize, swirl the pan to ensure even caramelization.

Continue to cook until a medium golden brown color. (Remember sugar syrup continues to cook after you remove it from the heat, so don't allow it to cook to too dark a color or else it will become bitter.)

Topping
continued

Remove the pan from the heat and with a wooden spoon in one hand, and the cream in the other, gradually pour the cream into the syrup, stirring constantly. The mixture will foam up and steam but will eventually become smooth.

Add butter and vanilla.

Cool until the caramel sauce thickens but can still be poured.

Spread over the cooled brownies and sprinkle with nuts.

Slice into squares or bars using a knife dipped into water and wiped clean after every slice.

Bridget Lunn
Private Caterer

"A piece of freshly cut baguette with a piece of bittersweet chocolate thrust into the middle of it was the daily *gouter* of the students who attended le Couvent du Sacré-Coeur in the northern industrial city of Metz, France. This simple and satisfying four o'clock ritual planted the seed in my nine-year-old heart of a longstanding affair with good food."

# Walnut-Black Pepper Biscotti

½ cup butter 112 g

1 cup sugar 200 g

2 eggs 2

1 ½ tsp vanilla 7 mL

1 tsp baking powder 5 mL

½ tsp baking soda 2 mL

pinch salt pinch

1 ½ tsp freshly ground black pepper 7 mL

1 orange rind 1 finely grated

1 lemon 1 rind finely grated

2 cups unbleached, all-purpose flour 280 g

1 ¼ cups walnuts 150 g toasted

sugar to garnish

**36 cookies**

Preheat oven to 350°F (180°C).

Cover a baking tray with parchment paper. Set aside.

In the bowl of an electric mixer fitted with the paddle attachment, beat the butter and sugar until fluffy.

Add the eggs 1 at a time until well blended. Scrape the sides of the bowl after each addition.

Add the vanilla, baking powder, baking soda and salt. Blend well.

Mix the pepper, orange and lemon rind with the flour. Add to the butter mixture, mixing only until completely blended.

Remove the bowl from the machine and fold in the toasted nuts by hand.

Dip your hands in some flour and divide the dough in half.

Form each half into a flat log, about 12 inches (30 cm) long and 3 inches (7.5 cm) wide.

Sprinkle with sugar.

Bake 20-25 minutes until light brown.

Cool out of the oven for 10 minutes.

With a serrated knife, slice the loaf into 1-inch (2.5-cm) slices.

Place cut-side down on baking sheet.

Return to the oven and bake an additional 15 minutes until golden brown and crisp.

Cool. Store in an airtight tin.

Lillian Kaplun

Mentor / Cooking
Teacher /
Cookbook Author

No baking section is complete without a classic sour cream coffee cake and this is it. I used to make this version, expanded considerably, for our hungry students who would visit BagelWorks opposite the University of Toronto. The key is to be sure that the butter is at room temperature and that it is beaten with the sugar at high speed not only until fluffy but until the mixture is almost white in appearance. Then, add the eggs one at a time, scraping the bottom and sides of the bowl before adding the next one. Your cake will rise high and be deliciously moist.

# Sour Cream Coffee Cake

## Topping

¼ cup brown sugar 55 g

1 tsp ground cinnamon 5 mL

2 Tbsp chopped nuts 50 g
   or to taste

## Batter

1 cup sour cream 250 mL

1 tsp baking soda 5 mL

2 cups cake flour 240 g

½ tsp salt 1 mL

2 tsp baking powder 2 mL

½ cup butter 112 g
   room temperature

1 cup less 2 Tbsp sugar 175 g

2 eggs 2
   room temperature

1 tsp vanilla 5 mL

**10 servings**

### Topping

Combine all ingredients and mix well. Set aside.

### Batter

Preheat oven to 350°F (180°C). Grease a 10-inch (25-cm) springform pan with vegetable spray.

In a medium bowl, combine sour cream and baking soda. Let stand while preparing the other ingredients.

Sift together flour, baking salt and powder.

In the bowl of an electric mixer fitted with the paddle attachment, cream the butter. Add sugar gradually and cream thoroughly for at least 10 minutes until light and fluffy, scraping the bowl often.

Add eggs 1 at a time, beating well and scraping the bowl after each addition.

Add vanilla and mix briefly.

Fold in sifted dry ingredients alternately with sour cream and baking soda.

Pour half of mixture into prepared pan. Smooth with a spatula.

Sprinkle with half the topping.

Pour on the rest of the batter. Smooth with a spatula.

Sprinkle with the remaining topping.

Bake for 40-45 minutes or until a toothpick tests clean and the center is puffed and firm to the touch.

Cool in pan then remove.

Joanne Yolles
Freelance Pastry
Chef

"This is actually a grown-up version of a childhood classic, although my seven-year-old is beginning to prefer this to the commercial variety. The ice cream is really a frozen mousse. It can simply be poured into a 6-cup (1.5-L) loaf pan and served in slices, or, as in this recipe, sandwiched between two thin layers of the still-tender-even-when-frozen chocolate cake. The chocolate cake recipe is inspired by the one in Paula Peck's classic, *The Art of Fine Baking*."

# Praline Ice Cream Sandwiches

## Chocolate Cake

6 oz semi-sweet chocolate 170 g
  in pieces

6 eggs 6
  separated

¾ cup sugar 150 g

2 Tbsp strong coffee 30 mL

1 tsp vanilla 5 mL

pinch salt pinch

¼ cup cocoa 30 g

## Frozen Praline Mousse

½ cup assorted nuts 60 g
  lightly toasted

½ cup sugar 100 g

2 Tbsp water 30 mL

6 eggs 6

¾ cup sugar 150 g

2 Tbsp cognac or brandy 30 mL

1 vanilla bean 1
  split

1 ¾ cup 35% whipping cream 435 mL

## Caramel Sauce

¾ cup sugar 150 g

½ cup water 125 mL

¼ cup 35% whipping cream 65 mL

**9 pieces**

### Chocolate Cake

Preheat oven to 375°F (180°C).

Line an 11-inch x 16-inch (28-cm x 40-cm) jelly roll pan with parchment paper.

Place chocolate in the top of a double boiler set over barely simmering water. Be sure that bottom of the bowl does not touch the water.

Stir frequently until chocolate is melted and smooth. Set aside to cool.

Place the egg yolks in a large bowl and set aside. Place the whites into the bowl of an electric mixer.

Using the whisk attachment beat the whites with a pinch of salt until they hold soft peaks.

Add the sugar in a very slow stream and beat until the whites form stiff peaks. Set aside.

Whisk egg yolks until smooth. Stir in coffee and vanilla and then melted chocolate.

Fold one quarter of the stiffly beaten egg whites into the chocolate mixture, and then gently fold in the remaining egg whites.

Pour into prepared pan and spread evenly.

Bake for 10 minutes. Reduce the heat to 350°F (160°C) and continue to bake about 5 minutes longer or until the top of the cake is firm. Cool in the pan.

**Frozen Praline Mousse**

Butter a baking sheet and set aside.

Coarsely chop the nuts.

Put the sugar and water in a small, heavy-bottomed saucepan. Swirl gently to moisten the sugar.

Over low heat, dissolve the sugar. Increase the heat and cook until it is a light caramel color.

Stir the nuts into the caramel and pour the mixture onto the buttered baking sheet. Allow to cool and harden.

Remove the praline from the baking sheet and transfer to a plastic bag. Using a mallet or rolling pin, pound the praline until it is broken into small chunks. Set aside.

In a large stainless steel bowl, whisk together the eggs, sugar and cognac.

Split the vanilla bean in half lengthwise. Scrap the black seeds into the egg mixture, then add the bean.

Place the bowl over a pot of simmering water and continuously whisk the mixture until very thick and hot to the touch, about 10 minutes. Place the bowl into another bowl filled with ice water and cool completely, whisking occasionally.

In the bowl of an electric mixer fitted with the whisk attachment, whip the cream on high speed to soft peaks; fold the whipped cream and the chopped praline into the egg mixture.

continued

# Praline Ice Cream Sandwiches (continued)

Assembly

Cut a sheet of wax paper the same length as the jelly roll pan. Sift the cocoa over the entire surface of the paper.

Turn out the cake on the cocoa-covered paper and carefully peel off the parchment paper.

Line a 9-inch (23-cm) square cake pan with plastic wrap or wax paper. Trim the edges of the cake and cut into 2 squares to fit the cake pan.

Using the bottom of a tart pan or a rimless cookie sheet, carefully transfer one of the cake squares to the pan. Fill with the praline mixture and top with the remaining cake square. Cover tightly with plastic wrap and freeze overnight.

Once frozen, turn out onto a cutting board, remove paper, and cut into individual servings.

Dust with a little more cocoa and/or icing sugar. Allow the sandwiches to soften slightly before serving. The flavor and texture will be more divine. Serve with Caramel Sauce for an extra treat.

Caramel Sauce

Put the sugar in a small, heavy-bottomed saucepan. Add half the water without stirring.

Over low heat, dissolve the sugar in the water.

Increase the heat to high and cook the sugar until it is a light caramel color. Reduce the heat to low; add remaining water and cream. Mixture will bubble up and steam. Stir until the sauce is smooth.

Remove from heat and cool.

Whisk thoroughly and serve or warm slightly. If sauce separates between uses, simply stir before serving. May be prepared 3 days in advance.

Leah Kalish

Leah's Home
Baking

One year, Leah outdid herself (as she usually does) by presenting a table filled with homemade candies. It was incredible to look at and incredibly popular with the sophisticated crowd. This is one of the bunch from that year.

# Caramel Popcorn

4 cups popped popcorn 1 L

½ tsp salt 2 mL

⅔ cup sugar 165 g

1/2 cup unsalted butter 112 g

¼ cup corn syrup 65 g

1 tsp vanilla 5 mL

**4-6 servings**

Salt popcorn.

Spread on ungreased cookie sheet.

Place sugar, butter and corn syrup in heavy saucepan over high heat.

Bring to a boil and insert a candy thermometer.

Boil until the syrup reaches 290°F (140°C).

Remove from the heat and stir in the vanilla.

Pour the syrup evenly over the popcorn.

Toss with 2 large spoons.

Cool. Store at room temperature.

Elaina Asselin

Whole Foods
Market

Elaina Asselin is one of the most talented Canadian chefs. She has worked at the remarkable Toqué in Montreal and the perennially feted Scaramouche in Toronto. She is equally at home creating elegant dishes as she is creating homey dishes such as this one. In her new position with Whole Foods Market where she is responsible for all the prepared food, a wider spectrum of the population will have access to her remarkable cuisine.

# Sticky Toffee Pudding

1 cup + 1 Tbsp unsalted butter 240 g

1 ½ cups brown sugar 300 g

1 cup + 3 Tbsp 35% whipping cream 300 mL

3 ¼ cups flour 400 g

1 tsp baking soda 5 mL

1 tsp baking powder 5 mL

pinch salt pinch

¾ + 1 Tbsp butter 185 g

1 ½ cups sugar 300 g

1 tsp vanilla 5 mL

6 large eggs 6

2 egg yolks 2

2 cups dried prunes 180 g diced

2 cups dried figs 180 g diced

### Butterscotch Rum Sauce

6 ½ Tbsp unsalted butter 90 g

1 cup dark brown sugar 220 g

2 Tbsp corn syrup 30 mL

⅓ cup 35% whipping cream 80 mL

⅔ cup dark rum 160 mL

**12 servings**

In a small saucepan, over medium heat, melt the butter, brown sugar and cream. Stir until smooth.

Set aside.

Preheat oven to 300°F (150°C).

Butter twelve 8-oz (227 mL) ramekins and set aside.

Mix the flour, baking soda, baking powder and salt together in a bowl. Set aside.

In the bowl of an electric mixer fitted with the paddle attachment, beat butter and sugar until fluffy. Add vanilla and blend.

Add eggs and egg yolks, 1 at a time, scraping down the sides of the bowl before each addition.

Add dry ingredients to the butter and eggs and mix until just blended.

Add the melted butter/brown sugar/cream mixture and blend gently.

Stir in dried fruits by hand.

Pour batter into prepared ramekins. Place them in a deep roasting pan.

Place the pan in the oven and pour boiling water three-quarters of the way up the sides of the ramekins.

Bake for approximately 2 hours or until the tops are puffed and springy.

Cool to set.

Serve warm, either in the ramekins, or reheat in a 250°F (120°C) oven for 15 minutes and unmold by running a thin knife around the edges.

Serve with Butterscotch Rum Sauce.

Butterscotch Rum Sauce

In a small saucepan, melt the butter.

Add sugar and corn syrup, stirring until the sugar is completely dissolved.

Add cream and blend.

Add dark rum and stir until blended.

Serve warm.

Dufflet Rosenberg
Dufflet Pastries

"This is one of my favorite creations where the finished cake is even more fabulous than the mere sum of its ingredients! I grew up with the classic sour cream coffee cake with cinnamon streusel so I played with it a little, taking it a delicious step further by adding English toffee (Skor bar chunks) to the batter, then topping it with a silken Milk Chocolate Glaze and homemade Caramel Drizzle. No one can stop at just one slice!"

# Toffee Sour Cream Coffee Cake

## Cake

1 ¾ cups sour cream 435 mL

1 tsp baking soda 5 mL

½ cup + 4 Tbsp unsalted butter 170 g
room temperature

1 ¾ cups sugar 350 g

3 eggs 3
room temperature

2 tsp vanilla 10 mL

3 cups all-purpose flour 420 g

1 ½ tsp baking powder 7 mL

1 cup Skor bars 170 g
broken into bits

1 cup pecans 125 g
lightly toasted, coarsely chopped

## Milk Chocolate Glaze

3 oz milk chocolate 85 g

¼ cup unsalted butter 56 g

## Caramel Drizzle

1 cup 35% whipping cream 250 mL

1 ¾ cups sugar 350 g

½ cup cold water 125 mL

5 Tbsp cold, unsalted butter 70 g
cubed

1 tsp vanilla 5 mL

pinch salt pinch

**10-12 servings**

## Cake

Preheat oven to 350°F (180°C).

Butter and flour a 9-inch (23-cm) tube pan.

Stir together sour cream and baking soda. Set aside.

Place butter and sugar in the bowl of an electric mixer fitted with the paddle attachment. On medium speed, cream together until light and fluffy.

Add eggs 1 at a time, incorporating and scraping down the sides before each addition.

Add vanilla and mix well.

Sift flour and baking powder together and add alternately with sour cream mixture to the batter in 3 additions.

Mix just until all the ingredients are blended.

Remove the bowl from the mixer and stir in Skor bar and pecan pieces.

Pour batter into the tube pan.

Bake for 50-60 minutes or until cake tester comes out clean. Cool in the pan before removing.

## Milk Chocolate Glaze

Place chocolate and butter together in a bowl over slowly simmering water.

Stir constantly until melted.

Remove from heat and allow to cool to room temperature.

## Caramel Drizzle

**Note**

This is more caramel sauce than you will need for the cake. Store in a sealed jar in the fridge for up to 3 weeks or more.

In a small saucepan, heat cream until small bubbles appear around the edges. Set aside.

In a medium saucepan, combine sugar and 1/2 cup (125 mL) cold water. Stir gently to moisten sugar.

Over medium heat, bring sugar to a simmer, swirling the pan gently to dissolve sugar.

Increase the heat and continue to simmer without stirring until the syrup begins to color.

Once the syrup turns a deep amber or caramel color, remove from the heat and add the cream in a steady stream, stirring with a wire whisk.

The caramel and cream will bubble up and steam, and may even clump, but keep stirring and continue to whisk until caramel is completely dissolved and combined with the cream into a smooth sauce-like consistency.

Stir in the pieces of butter until melted and thoroughly combined.

Add the vanilla and salt.

Set aside to cool.

## Assembly

Invert the cooled cake onto a serving platter.

Pour Milk Chocolate Glaze over cake so that it trickles down the sides.

Using a spatula, drizzle slightly warm caramel over the ganache.

Store cake covered at room temperature.

Joanne Yolles
Freelance Pastry
Chef

"Besides the famous Scaramouche Coconut Cream Pie, I've
made more of these chocolate cakes than any other
dessert. Whenever a birthday rolls around, this is the cake
I make. It is nice and chocolatey but also very light."

# Chocolate Layer Cake

## Chocolate Layers

6 oz semi-sweet chocolate 170 g
  chopped

½ cup boiling water 125 mL

2 ½ cups cake flour 300 g
  sifted

1 tsp baking powder 5 mL

1 tsp baking soda 5 mL

pinch salt pinch

1 cup butter 227 g
  room temperature

1 ½ cups sugar 300 g

1 tsp vanilla 5 mL

4 eggs 4
  room temperature, separated

1 cup buttermilk 250 mL

## Chocolate Cream

2 ½ cups 35% whipping cream
  625 mL

3 heaping Tbsp cocoa 35-40 g

3-4 heaping Tbsp sugar 65-70 g

**10-12 servings**

## Chocolate Layers

Preheat oven to 350°F (180°C). Grease the bottom of
three 9-inch (23-cm) layer cake pans. Line each bottom
with parchment paper.

Place chopped chocolate in a small bowl. Pour in boiling
water and stir until chocolate is melted and smooth. Set
aside to cool.

Sift together flour, baking powder, baking soda and salt.
Set aside.

In the bowl of an electric mixer fitted with the paddle
attachment cream the butter.

Add sugar gradually, beating well after each addition.
Add the vanilla and continue beating until creamy.

Add egg yolks 1 at a time. Beat well, scraping the bowl
with a rubber spatula as necessary to keep the mixture
smooth.

Add cooled chocolate and beat until combined.

On the lowest speed, alternately add dry ingredients in
4 additions and buttermilk in 3 additions, beating only
until smooth. Remove the bowl from the mixer.

In the bowl of an electric mixer fitted with the whisk
attachment beat the egg whites on high speed until
they are stiff but not dry.

Fold egg whites into chocolate cake batter.

Evenly divide the batter among the pans and spread the
tops level with an offset spatula.

Bake 30-35 minutes or until the tops spring back when
lightly touched and the cakes come away from the sides
of the pans.

Remove from the oven and cool in the pans for 5-10 minutes. Run a knife around the sides of the pans to release the cake layers. Cover each layer with a rack, invert, and remove pan and paper. Cool the layers completely before frosting.

Chocolate
Cream

In a large bowl, combine the whipping cream and the sugar. Sift in the cocoa.

Place the bowl and the whisk attachment in the freezer for 10 minutes.

On high speed, beat the cream until it holds its shape.

Place 1 cake layer on a serving platter protected with 4 strips of parchment paper set at right angles to one another, forming a square beneath the cake.

With a metal spatula, spread one quarter of the Chocolate Cream on the cake. Continue with remaining layers and Chocolate Cream.

Spread a thin layer of Chocolate Cream over the top and sides of the cake to set the crumbs. Chill for 5-10 minutes.

With a clean metal spatula, spread the remaining cream on the cake.

If there is extra cream, it can be used to pipe a border around the top of the cake.

Gently remove the paper strips.

Chill the cake but remove from the fridge at least 1 hour prior to serving. The cake layers can be prepared 1 day in advance (or frozen well wrapped in plastic and foil for up to 3 months) but frost the cake the day you plan to serve it.

Catherine O'Donnell
Pastry Chef
Hillebrand
Vineyard Café

# Chocolate Cheesecake

## Base

1 ½ cups Oreo cookies 150 g
crushed

4 ½ Tbsp butter 75 mL
melted

## Toffee Topping

1 can sweetened condensed milk
300 mL

¾ cup unsalted butter 170 g

3 Tbsp corn syrup 45 mL

¾ cup brown sugar 165 g

## Cheesecake Filling

2 ¼ lbs cream cheese 1 kg 20 g

¾ cup sugar 150 g

6 oz chocolate 170 g
melted

5 eggs 5

**2 cheesecakes**
10 servings each

### Base

Preheat oven to 350°F (180°C).

In the bowl of a food processor fitted with the steel blade, grind the cookies and add the melted butter.

Process just until crumbs are completely coated with butter.

Press into the bottom of two 10-inch (25-cm) spring-form pans.

Bake for 5 minutes. Cool on a wire rack.

### Toffee Topping

In a heavy-bottomed saucepan over medium heat, place all the topping ingredients.

Stir constantly while the mixture is coming to a boil. Once it is boiling, cook for 5 minutes to thicken.

Remove from heat and divide topping between the 2 bases.

### Cheesecake Filling

Preheat oven to 300°F (150°C).

In the bowl of an electric mixer fitted with the paddle attachment, mix cream cheese and sugar until completely smooth, about 5 minutes.

Gradually add eggs 1 at a time allowing them to be incorporated before adding the next one. Scrape the bowl often. Mix until completely smooth.

**Cheesecake
Filling**
continued

Pour some of the cream cheese batter into the melted chocolate, whisk together briefly and then pour the chocolate mixture back into the bowl with the cream cheese batter. Mix until thoroughly incorporated.

Pour the chocolate cream cheese batter into the spring-form pans.

Place pans in roasting pans with sides.

Place pans in the oven.

Bake for 35-40 minutes or until there is only a quarter-sized area in the very center of the filling that wobbles when the pan is gently jiggled.

Chill overnight before removing from pans.

Catherine O'Donnell
Pastry Chef
Hillebrand
Vineyard Café

# Chocolate Truffle Tart

½ lb unsalted butter 227 g

⅔ scant cup shortening 150 g

¾ cup sugar 150 g

1 ½ eggs 1 ½

1 Tbsp milk 15 mL

¼ tsp vanilla 1 mL

3 cups bread flour 420 g

½ cup cocoa 60 g

## Chocolate Truffle Tart Filling

½ cup butter 112 g

1 cup less 2 Tbsp dark chocolate 130 g
  chopped

½ cup sugar 100 g

3 egg yolks 3

1 ½ tsp brandy 7 mL

2 ½ Tbsp water 35 mL

1 tsp coffee extract 5 mL

½ cup 35% whipping cream 125 mL

**10 servings**

In the bowl of an electric mixer fitted with the paddle attachment, cream the butter, shortening and sugar.

Add the eggs all at once with the milk and vanilla. Beat on medium speed, scraping the sides of the bowl to achieve a homogeneous mixture.

Add flour and cocoa and mix until completely incorporated.

Pat into a round disc. Wrap in plastic and refrigerate for 15 minutes.

Preheat oven to 350°F (180°C).

On a lightly floured surface, roll out the dough to 1/8-inch (.3-cm) thickness, and 12-inch (30-cm) diameter.

Carefully lift the dough and place it in a 10-inch (25-cm) fluted pie tin with a removable bottom.

Gently push the overhanging dough down the sides.

Trim the edges and gently press the dough into the sides of the pan.

Chill for 10-15 minutes prior to baking. Wrap and freeze any leftover dough.

Bake for 10-15 minutes or until dough is beginning to firm up.

Prick the dough in a few places with a fork, and return the tart shell to the oven for an additional 10 minutes or until it feels dry to the touch. Be careful not to over-bake. Remove and cool on a wire rack.

**Chocolate Truffle Tart Filling**

Place butter and chocolate in a bowl set over a pan of barely simmering water.

When butter and chocolate are completely melted remove from heat.

In a separate bowl, combine sugar and egg yolks. Whisk until mixture reaches body temperature.

Pour the eggs into the chocolate mixture and whisk well.

Add the brandy, water and coffee extract. Cool for about 15 minutes.

Set aside one quarter of the filling for the topping.

Pour remaining filling into the chocolate flan shell.

Chill.

In the bowl of an electric mixer fitted with the whisk attachment, whip cream until medium peaks form.

Gently fold in the remaining truffle filling and either pipe rosettes around the border or drop evenly by tablespoons in dramatic mounds on top of the tart.

Chill. Remove from the refrigerator about 15 minutes prior to serving.

Catherine O'Donnell

Pastry Chef
Hillebrand
Vineyard Café

"This is a nifty recipe with a fabulous-looking result but you need to have a few special tools on hand, namely: three stainless steel tubes 2 inches (5 cm) in diameter and approximately 2 1/2 inches (7 cm) tall. These will serve as molds for the white chocolate center. If you can't find or don't want to go looking for them, suitable substitutes would be three tomato paste cans with both bottoms cut out, washed and dried."

# Chocolate Macadamia Terrine

## White Center

1 ¼ cup white chocolate 185 g
    chopped

½ cup less 1 Tbsp 35% whipping cream
    100 mL

1 ½ Tbsp raspberry liqueur 22 mL

½ cup macadamia nuts 65 g
    toasted, finely chopped

## Dark Outer Layer

1 cup bittersweet chocolate 150 g
    chopped

½ cup 35% whipping cream 125 mL

2 Tbsp maple syrup 30 mL

fresh berries, mint to garnish

8 servings

### Day One

Place the white chocolate in a small bowl. Place the cream in a small saucepan and heat to just below boiling.

Pour the cream over the chocolate and let rest for 10 minutes.

Stir briskly to melt all the chocolate. If some bits remain, place the bowl over barely simmering hot water until the chocolate is smooth. Do not let the chocolate get too hot.

Add the raspberry liqueur, blend and add the macadamia nuts.

Set the stainless steel tubes on a cookie sheet and divide the white chocolate evenly among them.

Place in the freezer overnight.

### Day Two

Line one 8-inch x 4-inch (20-cm x 10-cm) bread pan with parchment paper overhanging the long sides by 3 inches (7.5 cm).

Unmold the white chocolate terrine centers by holding a towel dipped in hot water around the outside of the tube. Gently push the white chocolate so that it slides out.

With a thin, sharp knife, cut the white chocolate tube in half from top to bottom so that you have two half-moon-shaped pieces. Return to freezer until ready to use.

Place dark chocolate in a small stainless steel bowl.

**Day Two**
continued

Heat the whipping cream to just below boiling and pour over the chocolate. Let rest 10 minutes.

Stir briskly to melt all the chocolate. If some bits remain, place the bowl over some barely simmering hot water until the chocolate is smooth. Do not let the chocolate get too hot.

Fill the prepared pan with half the dark chocolate.

Place the white chocolate half moons round side down into the chocolate and end to end down the length of the pan. Press gently into the dark chocolate.

Pour the rest of the dark chocolate into the terrine, spreading it evenly to cover the filling.

Place the terrine in the freezer for 8 hours.

When ready to serve, place a serving platter on top of the terrine and invert. The terrine will fall out of the pan. Remove the paper. Surround with fresh berries and sprigs of mint.

To slice, use a thin, sharp knife, dipped in hot water and wiped dry.

Ayoma Fonseka

**Ayoma Cake Masterpieces**

Ayoma served several varieties of chocolate truffles when she first participated in Eat to the Beat. Now guests beat a hasty path to her table whenever they see her creations!

# Kahlúa Truffles

½ cup 35% whipping cream 125 mL

15 oz bittersweet chocolate 240 g
  chopped

1 Tbsp Kahlúa 15 mL

2 Tbsp butter 28 g

1 pound bittersweet chocolate 454 g
  melted, for dipping truffle centers

1 cup cocoa 120 g
  (optional)

**approximately 48 truffles**

Place cream into a medium saucepan and bring to a boil. Boil for 1 minute.

Remove from heat and add chopped chocolate. Stir until completely melted and smooth. Stir in the Kahlúa and butter. The mixture will be very runny.

Refrigerate for 30-50 minutes until firm.

Using a small ice cream scoop or a teaspoon, scoop the truffle filling and roll quickly and gently into balls.

Using a chocolate dipping fork or a regular fork, dip the centers into the melted chocolate and gently roll them off the end of the fork and onto the parchment-lined pan.

Once all the truffle filling has been dipped, you may re-dip them for a more professional finish or you may gently roll them in cocoa for a more rustic look.

# chapter 2

# appetizers

The second Eat to the Beat sold an amazing 500 tickets. Word had clearly spread that this event was worth attending, so despite the inclement weather people came in droves ... so many people, in fact, that there were lines of cars looking for parking spaces all over the residential area surrounding Casa Loma. Neighbors were not pleased.

There were lines, too, at the now better-organized (or so we thought!) cash bar, and the then very trendy martini bar.

Of course, there were lines as well at the tables of the new chefs offering bite-sized savories, which were followed by even more lines at the dessert tables.

We had become a victim of our own success and while people simply loved the event, they were quite vocal (albeit patient) about waiting on too many lines. It was time to seek a new venue.

You don't have to get in line to try these recipes. Jump around the chapter and sample them all. The recipes are all easy and no-nonsense. No one likes to spend a lot of time on fussy appetizers that are "scarfed" up as soon as guests arrive. Most of these recipes can be done up ahead of time and served at your leisure. One or two require some last minute assembly, but the outcome is well worth the effort.

Do try them!

Bridget Lunn
Private Caterer

"Country terrines generally require a combination of meats, spices, and herbs with a generous amount of pork back fat, which binds moisture, flavor and richness to the final product. During a menopause-induced memory lapse, I forgot to buy this essential fat and was forced to use my imagination to fill in the blank. The result is a lean terrine for the metabolically challenged baby boomer and is an example of how a disaster can be turned into a triumph."

# Boomer Lean Terrine

¼ lb lean veal 112 g
chopped by hand

8-9 oz lean pork 225-250 g

2 Tbsp shallots 30 g
finely chopped

2 Tbsp brandy 30 mL

1 Tbsp 35% whipping cream 15 mL

1 egg 1

1 Tbsp fresh thyme 15 mL
finely minced

½ tsp black pepper 2 mL
freshly ground

¼ tsp nutmeg 1 mL
freshly grated

pinch ground allspice pinch

1 medium green apple 1
(185 g peeled, cored and grated)

⅓ cup fresh or frozen cranberries 80 mL
or 1 oz dried shiitake mushrooms 28 g
soaked in hot water for 20 minutes
and thinly sliced

2 bay leaves 2

unsalted butter to grease pan

**4 servings**

Combine all the ingredients and mix well to blend.

Refrigerate overnight to allow flavors to meld.

Preheat oven to 350°F (180°C).

Butter a small 4-cup (1-L) terrine or bread pan.

Pack the mixture into prepared pan.

Place bay leaves on top.

Cover with buttered foil.

Place in a larger pan with 4-inch (10-cm) sides and fill with boiling water 3/4 of the way up the terrine.

Bake for approximately 1 1/2 hours until the internal temperature reaches 160°F (70°C).

Cool. Place a weight on top of the foil and refrigerate overnight.

Remove weight and foil, and pour off accumulated juices.

With a paper towel, wipe off any foam.

Store for up to 2 days in the refrigerator.

Serve with a green salad, country breads and a dried cherry chutney.

Dinah Koo

Tiger Lily's

"For more than 25 years, I have brought my unique enter-taining style to countless repeat customers, creating events for every possible occasion in every conceivable venue. In 1994 my restaurant Tiger Lily's, located on trendy Queen Street West, opened to provide a broader stage for my pan-Asian foods. Authentic egg rolls, noodle soups infused with my homemade stocks, and specially created noodle plates using only the freshest ingredients are just a few of our most popular items."

# Beef and Spinach Rolls

## Teriyaki Sauce

1/4 cup soy sauce 65 mL

1 1/2 tsp sherry 7 mL

2 Tbsp brown sugar 30 g

1/2 tsp crushed garlic 2 mL

1 tsp grated ginger 5 mL

2 tsp sesame oil 10 mL

**Yield** Scant 1/2 cup (125 mL)

## Beef & Spinach Rolls

1 lb beef tenderloin center cut 454 g
  frozen

8 sheets wax or parchment paper
  8 sheets
  cut 12 inches x 14 inches
  (30 cm x 36 cm)

1 10-oz bag spinach 280 g
  picked, washed, blanched and cooled

1/2 cup Teriyaki Sauce 125 mL

2 Tbsp sesame seeds 30 mL
  lightly toasted

30 toothpicks 30

**24 servings**

### Teriyaki Sauce

Mix all ingredients well. Set aside.

### Beef & Spinach Rolls

Partially thaw beef overnight in fridge. Beef must still be frozen but not rock hard since you must be able to slice it with a sharp knife.

Slice beef into 1/4-inch (.6-cm) thick pieces and place on a piece of parchment paper, slightly overlapping pieces in a row 10 inches (24 cm) long.

Place beef in freezer, until firm. Remove layer of paper.

Place a second piece of parchment paper on top of the beef. Press beef gently with fingers until an even thickness is attained. Do not press too hard—this could create holes.

Cut bottom lengthwise off beef slices to make an even edge.

Spread evenly with 1 tsp (5 mL) of Teriyaki Sauce.

Add an even layer of spinach and spread with an additional 1 tsp (5 mL) of Teriyaki Sauce.

Sprinkle with 1/2 tsp (2 mL) of sesame seeds.

Roll from the bottom, long edge, into a cigar shape, cutting top edge to make it even.

Evenly space 6 toothpicks along the roll and cut between them to make 6 beef rolls.

Using a non-stick skillet moistened with a bit of oil and set over very high heat, sauté beef rolls approximately 30 seconds on each side.

Drizzle with any remaining Teriyaki Sauce and sprinkle with toasted sesame seeds.

Repeat with remaining rolls and serve immediately.

Claire Stubbs
Mildred Pierce
Restaurant

Claire has been the Executive Chef at Mildred Pierce Restaurant for six years. She holds a degree in Film and English from Queen's University in Kingston, Ontario and attended the Stratford Chef's School, graduating with distinction. She apprenticed at the world renowned Sooke Harbour House in British Columbia before settling down at Mildred Pierce, where she creates constantly innovative and fun menus. Recently, she joined the team at The Cookworks where she is a chef instructor for cooking classes and corporate events.

# Cheddar Shortbreads
## with Red Pepper Jelly

### Shortbread Dough

1 tsp cayenne pepper 5 mL

1 tsp paprika 5 mL

1 tsp salt 5 mL

2 ½ cups all-purpose flour 350 g

½ lb unsalted butter 227 g
softened

½ lb cheddar cheese 227 g
grated

### Red Pepper Jelly

3 large red peppers 3
(400 g seeded, minced in food processor)

1 large red pepper 200 g
seeded, chopped by hand

5 ½ cups sugar 1 kg + 100 g

1 cup white vinegar 250 mL

⅓ cup lemon juice 85 mL

1 pkg pectin 57 g

3 dozen

Shortbread Dough

Preheat oven to 350°F (180°C). Line a baking sheet with parchment paper.

In a medium bowl sift together the cayenne, paprika, salt and flour.

In the bowl of an electric mixer fitted with the paddle attachment, beat butter until soft and light. Add cheddar cheese, mixing to combine.

Add dry ingredients gradually and mix well.

Roll dough into a cylinder 1 inch (2.5 cm) thick. Wrap in plastic wrap. Refrigerate for 1 hour until firm.

Slice into discs 1/4 inch (.6 cm) thick. Place on prepared baking sheet. Bake for 20-25 minutes, or until lightly golden.

Cool on a wire rack.

Red Pepper Jelly

Place red peppers in a deep stainless steel pot. Add sugar and vinegar. Bring to a boil, stirring constantly.

Remove from heat and cool for 15 minutes.

Bring to the boil again and add lemon juice. Boil at a full rolling boil for 2 minutes.

Remove from heat and stir in pectin.

Return to boil and continue to cook on a rolling simmer for 20 minutes.

Skim the surface for foam and impurities.

Cool slightly and bottle in prepared jars. Allow to set for 1 hour.

To serve, sandwich a little red pepper jelly between 2 shortbreads.

Claire Stubbs
**Mildred Pierce
Restaurant**

# Chèvre and Roasted Red Peppers
## Baked in Vine Leaves

2 large red peppers 400 g

1 jar grape vine leaves 500 mL

1 lb creamy chèvre 454 g
   in a log

olive oil

focaccia

extra-virgin olive oil

**6 servings**

Preheat oven to 350°F (180°C).

Place red peppers on a baking sheet and roast in the oven for 30 minutes. Transfer peppers to a bowl, cover tightly with plastic wrap and allow to steam for about 10 minutes.

Peel skin from peppers, removing seeds and stems and discarding. Cut the roasted pepper into 1/2-inch (1.2-cm) wide strips, about 6 strips per pepper.

Drain brine from vine leaves and rinse in lots of cold water. Set aside in a colander and let excess water run off leaves.

Use cheese wire or fishing line to cut the log of chèvre into 6 equal portions (dental floss will work too).

Place 1 vine leaf on your work surface and spread it out flat. Pat dry with a clean cloth or paper towel.

Overlap 2 or 3 more leaves until the leaves form a circle, no larger than 8 inches (20 cm) across. Pat these dry.

Place 1 portion of chèvre in the center of the leaves. Wrap strips of roasted pepper around the edge of the chèvre. Fold up the leaves around the chèvre and pepper to make a little parcel.

Preheat the oven to 375°F (190°C).

In a skillet set over high heat, pour in 1 Tbsp (15 mL) olive oil and swirl to cover the bottom of the pan.

Sear chèvre packages quickly on both sides and place on a baking sheet.

Bake for 5 minutes.

To serve, fold back the vine leaves to expose the soft chèvre and peppers.

Serve with warm focaccia and a drizzle of good olive oil.

Anna Olson
On the Twenty

"This appetizer was a big hit at Eat to the Beat 2001, and as the event was before Thanksgiving, a number of people asked for the recipe to prepare for their family dinner over the holidays. The recipe works well as a single tart to be cut into wedges and served, or also presents well as individual tarts."

# Sweet Potato Parmesan Tarts

## Crust

1 cup breadcrumbs 130 g

⅓ cup Parmesan cheese 75 mL grated

1 ¼ Tbsp fresh rosemary 19 mL chopped

dash black pepper dash

6 Tbsp butter 90 mL melted

1 egg yolk 1

## Filling

¾ lb sweet potatoes 340 g halved

2 tsp vegetable oil 10 mL

2 shallots 30 g minced

2 tsp fresh sage 10 mL chopped

to taste salt and pepper to taste

dash cayenne pepper dash

½ cup 35% whipping cream 125 mL

2 eggs 2

### Crust

Preheat oven to 350°F (180°C).

In a bowl, stir together breadcrumbs, Parmesan, rosemary and pepper.

Add melted butter and egg yolk and blend with fingers until crumbly, like a cheesecake crust.

Spoon mixture into 6 individual tart shells or a 9-inch (23-cm) pie plate. Press down firmly on crumbs to make them even.

Bake for 8 minutes until edges are golden brown. Remove and cool on a wire rack.

### Filling

Preheat oven to 350°F (180°C).

Prepare sweet potato by placing flesh-side down on a lightly oiled baking sheet.

Prick skin with a fork and bake until tender, about 30 minutes. Let cool.

Spoon out cooked sweet potato flesh and purée in a food processor or hand blender.

Heat vegetable oil in a small sauté pan over medium heat and sauté shallots for 3 minutes until tender.

Stir shallots and sage into sweet potato and season with salt, pepper and dash of cayenne.

Stir in cream and eggs.

Spread filling into tart shells and bake for 15 minutes, until you see the edges of the tart begin to soufflé.

Tart is best served warm, but can be served at room temperature.

### Vinaigrette

1 shallot 1
minced

1 1/2 tsp Dijon mustard 7 mL

4 Tbsp fresh lemon juice 60 mL

1 tsp fresh thyme 5 mL
chopped

4 Tbsp pumpkin seed oil 60 mL

1/3 cup vegetable oil 85 mL

2 Tbsp warm water 30 mL

to taste salt and pepper to taste

3 cups autumn greens 750 mL
such as watercress, radicchio,
Belgian endive and escarole
washed and dried

**6 portions**

### Vinaigrette

Whisk together in a small bowl the shallot, mustard, lemon juice and thyme.

Slowly whisk in the pumpkinseed oil until incorporated and repeat with vegetable oil.

Whisk in water and season to taste.

### Assembly

To serve tart, arrange greens on a salad plate and dress with vinaigrette.

Place warm tart atop greens.

The greens will wilt slightly, but this tenderizes them.

Joan Monfaredi

Executive Chef
Park Hyatt Hotel

"Growing up with a Ukranian grandma meant growing up with perogies. She always cooked the potatoes first and reserved the cooking water for the dough. This was a habit left from the days when she had no running water. In today's terms, it still makes sense because the nutrients from the potatoes are not poured down the drain. To this day, my dad refuses to eat perogies made by anyone except my mom or myself because when he was a boy he saw a neighbor make the perogies stick by licking the dough!"

# Perogies

### Potato Filling

8 medium red potatoes 2 kg

2 Tbsp salt 30 mL

12 oz aged cheddar 335 g
    grated

2 oz blue cheese 56 g
    mashed

to taste salt and pepper to taste

### Perogy Dough

4 cups all-purpose flour 560 g

1 tsp salt 5 mL

2 eggs 2
    beaten

1 ⅓ cups potato water 330 g
    room temperature

1 Tbsp vegetable oil 15 mL

water

butter for tossing

sour cream for serving

### 80 perogies

Potato Filling

Peel, drain, and quarter the potatoes.

Place in a large pot and cover with water. Add 2 Tbsp (30 mL) salt.

Bring to a boil and cook until fork tender.

Over a bowl, drain potatoes completely and mash with ricer or a masher, retaining the water for the dough.

Add both cheeses to the potatoes and mix well with a wooden spoon.

Taste for seasoning and add salt and pepper to taste.

Cool completely before making the perogies.


Perogy Dough

Place flour and salt in a large mixing bowl.

Combine eggs, water and oil and blend.

Pour into the flour and mix well by hand.

Turn out onto work surface and knead until dough is smooth and no longer sticky, 7-10 minutes. Add a bit more flour if the dough is too sticky.

Cover with plastic and let rest at room temperature at least 1 hour.

Divide dough into quarters and cover with plastic wrap while you roll each piece.

Roll one quarter to between 1/8–1/4-inch (.3–.6-cm) thick.

Cut into 3-inch (7.5-cm) squares.

Lift one square at a time and place down-side-up in the palm of your hand.

**Perogy Dough**
continued

Use a teaspoon to place a mound of potatoes in the center of the square.

Wet the edges of the dough lightly with water.

Bring the opposite sides together to form a triangle. Pinch the edges together to seal.

Bring a pot of salted water to the boil.

Boil the perogies for approximately 3 minutes.

Remove, drain, and toss with a little butter.

Serve with sour cream.

Jan Sherk
Word of Mouth
Cuisine

Jan Sherk is one of the many trained professional women who we would never have discovered if it hadn't been for one of our committee members, Janey McLeod, who used her to cater her parties. Jan doesn't advertise and devotes herself to an exclusive clientele who like to think she is their best kept secret … and she was, until she joined Eat to the Beat. Now everyone knows how to find this perfectionist who is best known not only for her food but for the creative backgrounds on which it is served: wild rice, lentils, beans, to name just a few items, line her platters and serve as inventive "doilies" that accent her delicious food.

# Black and White Sesame Chicken

4 chicken breasts 500 g
  boneless, skinless

to taste salt and pepper to taste

1 egg 1
  lightly beaten

⅓ cup water 80 mL

2 Tbsp + 1 tsp all-purpose flour 20 g

½ cup sesame seeds 80 g

½ cup black sesame seeds 80 g

1 ½ tsp Hungarian paprika 7 mL

⅓ cup canola oil 80 mL


**Chipotle Aioli Dip**

1 egg yolk 1

2 tsp lemon juice 10 ml

1 tsp apple cider vinegar 5 mL

1 clove garlic 5 g
  finely chopped

½, or more chipotle pepper in adobe
  sauce ½, or more
  finely chopped

⅓ cup + 1 Tbsp olive oil 95 mL

to taste salt and pepper to taste

Yield Serves 12 as a dip


**4 servings**

Rub chicken breasts with salt and pepper and let sit for 15 minutes.

Cut each breast into 1 1/2-inch (3.8-cm) cubes.

Beat the egg with the water in a shallow bowl.

In a plastic bag, combine the flour, sesame seeds, paprika and salt to taste, mixing well.

Place the chicken pieces in the egg mixture and coat on all sides.

Place the chicken in the plastic bag with the sesame mixture and toss to coat evenly.

Remove the chicken pieces from the bag and place on a cookie cooling rack.

Press down firmly on each chicken piece to make it flat and oval. If it isn't flattened it won't cook evenly.

Place in the fridge and let dry for a minimum of 1 hour.

In a deep frying pan, heat the oil to 350°F (180°C).

Deep-fry the chicken, turning only once.

Drain on a rack and blot with paper towels.

The chicken may be made 1 day in advance and refrigerated. Reheat in a 350°F(180°C) oven.

Serve with Chipotle Aioli Dip.

Chipotle Aioli Dip

For a quicker version substitute 1/3 cup (80 mL) Hellman's mayonnaise for the egg yolk, lemon juice, cider vinegar and the first quantity of olive oil. Proceed with the recipe from there. [But just once, you should make the homemade version of Jan's mayonnaise to learn what it should really taste like! Ed.]

In the bowl of a food processor fitted with the steel blade combine all the ingredients except olive oil, salt and pepper.

Pulse until blended.

With machine running, pour the oil in a slow but steady stream through the lid. The mixture will lighten in color and thicken up although it will not arrive at the consistency of store-bought mayonnaise.

Add more chipotles if it is not hot enough.

Adjust seasoning.

Suzanne Baby
Gallery Grill at
Hart House

Born in Toronto, Suzanne Baby points to her upbringing in a food-savvy French-Canadian home as the spark that ignited her passion for great-tasting cuisine. She apprenticed at Stockholm's famous Uto Bageri restaurant after which she completed her culinary management degree with stints at the Windsor Arms Hotel, Bistro 990, Splendido and Lakes Bar and Grill before finally calling the University of Toronto's Hart House Grill home.

# BBQ Duck in Scallion Crepes

## BBQ Duck

1, 5 lb whole duck 1, 2 kg
  cleaned

to taste salt and pepper to taste

1 medium onion 200 g
  coarsely chopped

2 medium carrots 200 g
  coarsely chopped

3 cups hoisin sauce 750 mL

½ cup brown sugar 110 g

2 Tbsp ground coriander 30 mL

1 Tbsp anise seed 15 mL

½ tsp chili flakes 2 mL

½ tsp Chinese 5 spice powder 2 mL

¼ tsp cayenne pepper 1 mL

## Scallion Crepes

3 eggs 3

1 ¼ cups milk 315 mL

1 ¼ tsp salt 3 mL

½ tsp sesame oil 2 mL

¾ cup all-purpose flour 105 g

¼ cup finely chopped scallions 40 g

½ tsp black sesame seeds 2 mL

vegetable oil for brushing on pan

8 servings

## BBQ Duck

Preheat oven to 375°F (190°C).

Rinse duck and dry well.

Season generously with salt and pepper.

Place onion and carrots in the bottom of roasting pan. Add enough water to cover vegetables halfway.

Place duck on the vegetables and roast for approximately 1 1/2 to 2 hours, or until the duck is tender but not dried out.

Remove the legs and breast, keeping them as intact as possible.

Trim off any unrendered fat.

Remove any remaining meat from the carcass and set aside.

Mix hoisin sauce with remaining ingredients.

Brush enough sauce on duck breasts and legs to cover. Reserve remainder.

BBQ the duck pieces on a hot grill or broil until the top is caramelized but not burned.

## Scallion Crepes

Whisk together eggs, milk, salt, and sesame oil.

Put flour into bowl of food processor fitted with the steel blade.

With processor running, add liquid ingredients. Process until smooth.

**Scallion Crepes**
continued

Strain mixture into a bowl. Cover and refrigerate for a minimum of 1 hour.

Stir in scallions and sesame seeds.

Heat a 6-inch (15-cm) crepe or frying pan. Brush lightly with vegetable oil.

The first crepe is usually a mess but don't worry.

Pour 1/4 cup (65 mL) of batter into the center of the pan and swirl it around so that the batter covers the bottom in a thin veil.

Flip the crepe when the bottom side is lightly speckled with brown dots.

Cook the second side only long enough to remove any raw batter. The crepes should remain pliable and not be crispy.

Stack on a plate.

**Assembly**

Remove meat from leg bone and shred breast and leg meat together with smaller pieces of meat removed from the whole duck.

Toss with 4-5 Tbsp (60-70 mL) of hoisin mixture and reheat gently.

Place heated duck meat in crepes.

Roll crepes, place in a shallow pan, cover with foil and reheat for 2-3 minutes.

Jan Sherk
Word of Mouth
Cuisine

# Papaya Guacamole with Taro Chips

## Guacamole

1 small papaya 1
    peeled, seeded and diced into
    ¼-inch (.6-cm) pieces

⅛ red onion 65 g
    finely diced

1 ½ plum tomatoes 175 g
    seeded, diced

1 jalapeño pepper 20 g
    seeded, minced

1 Tbsp fresh cilantro 15 mL
    chopped

to taste salt and pepper to taste

2 lbs taro 1 kg
    peeled

to taste salt to taste

4 cups canola oil 1 L

1 avocado 1
    ripe

1 ½ Tbsp lime juice 20 mL

## Taro Chips

2 taro tubers 2

vegetable oil for deep frying

to taste salt to taste

Yield 60 chips

**15 servings**

### Guacamole

Prepare all the ingredients except avocado and lime juice and layer in a container.

Just before serving, pour the lime juice into a small bowl. Peel and dice the avocado right into the lime juice. Mix.

Fold avocado and lime juice into the layered ingredients. Season according to taste, adding more salt or lime juice as required.

### Taro Chips

In a deep, heavy-bottomed saucepan, heat the oil to 325°F (160°C).

Peel the taro roots 1 at a time and slice across the grain, very thinly, on a mandoline set over a towel. Slice only as many as you can fry at one time.

Drop the chips into the hot oil, being careful not to crowd them.

Fry until they are golden brown on both sides, turning them once so that they don't burn.

Slice the next batch while the first batch is cooking.

Drain on paper towels and season with a light sprinkling of salt.

Elaina Asselin

**Whole Foods
Market**

This is another example of Elaina's simple but gutsy cooking that is full of flavor and quick to assemble.

# Sautéed Calamari and Spicy Sausage

1 Tbsp olive oil 15 mL

1.5 lbs squid 750 g
   cleaned and sliced into rings

to taste salt and pepper to taste

3-4 cloves garlic 3-4

1 leek 1
   washed, and thinly sliced into rounds

6 shiitake mushrooms 6
   sliced

1 merguez, chorizo or spicy Italian
   sausage 1
   sliced

¼ cup orange juice 65 mL

1-2 Tbsp balsamic vinegar 15-30 mL

fresh basil to garnish

**4 servings**

In a medium sauté pan, heat olive oil over high heat.

Season squid with salt and pepper.

Sauté squid in hot oil for 2-3 minutes. Remove from pan. Lower heat.

Add leeks and shiitake mushrooms and stir for 2-3 minutes. Remove and set aside with squid.

Add sausage to the pan and cook until caramelized on all sides. Remove from pan and set aside.

Deglaze pan with orange juice, scraping up whatever crispy bits remain. Add balsamic vinegar to taste.

Add squid, leeks, mushrooms, and sausage and reheat quickly.

Serve immediately, garnished with fresh basil.

Anne Yarymowich

**The Agora** at the
**Art Gallery of Ontario**

"Every chef has an ingredient they tend to overuse. Mine is salt cod. My fascination with salt cod began when I first came across this seemingly inedible product at Kensington Market. What was this hard, dry fish, and what did one do with it? My curiosity led me to research this intriguing ingredient so integral to Mediterranean cuisine. I came across this recipe in a little cookbook called *Potager*. I have adapted it slightly and it has become a favorite."

# Salt Cod Gratin

2 lbs salt cod 1 kg

3 cloves garlic 15 g

3 bay leaves 3

2 cups leeks 160 g
  finely chopped

4 Tbsp less 1 tsp butter 50 g

4 Tbsp + 1 tsp olive oil 65 mL

to taste salt, cayenne pepper, pepper
  to taste

1 ¼ cups Gruyere cheese 150 g
  grated

### Bechamel Sauce

4 Tbsp less 1 tsp butter 50 g

5 Tbsp + 2 tsp flour 50 g

2 cups whole milk 500 mL

### Garnish

10 cured black olives 10

¼ bunch Italian parsley sprigs ¼ bunch

baguette, pita or lavash to serve

**8 servings**

Pre-soak salt cod for a minimum of 24 hours, changing water as often as possible. The amount of soaking will vary depending on the saltiness of the cod.

In a large pot, cover the soaked, rinsed cod with fresh cold water.

Add the garlic cloves and bay leaves. Bring to the boil and reduce heat to low. Simmer until the fish flakes to the touch.

Remove from the water and let cool.

When cool, separate into small flakes, discarding bay leaves and garlic cloves. Set aside to cool completely.

Sweat the leeks gently in butter and olive oil, seasoning lightly with salt, cayenne and pepper.

Add the flaked cod and toss gently to blend.

Preheat oven to 375°F (190°C).

In a medium saucepan, melt the butter and add the flour. Whisk together to make a blond roux.

Whisk in the milk gradually, while stirring constantly over medium heat until the sauce has thickened.

Remove from the heat and let cool.

Mix together the bechamel, grated Gruyere and the leek and cod mixture. Pour into 1 large buttered gratin dish or 8 buttered ramekins.

Dot with butter and bake for 10-20 minutes or until the tops are golden and bubbling.

Garnish with cured black olives and a sprig of Italian parsley.

Serve with toasted baguette, warm pita or crisp lavash.

Lili Sullivan
Freelance Chef

Lili is known for her earthy, forthright cooking. She is unafraid to combine ingredients that might seem out of place together to create something totally imaginative, or to take a familiar item and turn it into something magnificent like this rich appetizer cheesecake.

# Savory Crab and Almond Cheesecake

**Crust**

scant ½ cup breadcrumbs 60 g

4 tsp coarsely ground almonds 15 g

1 Tbsp melted butter 15 mL


½ lb crabmeat 227 g

1 lb cream cheese 454 g

1 cup blanched almonds 160 g

2 green onions 2
  finely chopped

2 stalks celery 80 g
  finely chopped

1 Tbsp horseradish 15 mL

1 lemon 30 mL
  juiced

1 Tbsp Worcestershire sauce 15 mL

1 tsp mustard powder 5 mL

3 eggs 3

½ cup 35% whipping cream 125 mL


**Topping**

1 cup sour cream 250 mL

1 cup toasted, sliced almonds 160 g


**14-16 appetizer servings**

In a small bowl, combine all crust ingredients. Press into bottom of a 10-inch (25-cm) springform pan.

Preheat oven to 400°F (200°C).

In a food processor fitted with the steel blade, purée crabmeat, cream cheese, almonds, green onions, and celery until smooth.

Add remaining ingredients and blend well. Pour into prepared pan.

Bake for about 40 minutes or until sides are puffy and middle of cheesecake is set.

Cool at room temperature for 1 hour and then in the fridge for at least 8 hours or overnight before slicing.

Spread sour cream overtop cheesecake and sprinkle with almonds before serving.

Virginia Marr

Executive Chef
Pillar and Post
Niagara-on-
the-Lake

To my mind, potatoes and smoked salmon were made for
one another. But add some goat cheese and crisp the potatoes and you have a whole new dimension. Although this is in
the appetizer category, it could just as well be served for
brunch.

# Smoked Bay of Fundy Salmon Potato Flapjack Stack

### Potato Flapjacks

4 Yukon Gold potatoes 800 g
   washed, peeled, and shredded

pinch nutmeg pinch
   freshly grated

to taste salt and pepper to taste

4 Tbsp olive oil 60 mL

### Salmon Stack

8 slices smoked salmon 8

4 oz herbed goat cheese 112 g

1 lemon rind 1
   finely grated

2 cups mesclun lettuce 500 mL

1 tsp tarragon vinegar 5 mL

1 Tbsp extra virgin olive oil 15 mL

### Assembly

4 Tbsp 35% cream 60 mL
   whipped to soft peaks

chives chopped

caviar of your choice

**4 servings**

### Potato Flapjacks

In a medium bowl, mix together the shredded potato,
nutmeg and salt and pepper.

In a non-stick frying pan set on medium heat, heat the
olive oil.

Spoon 1 or 2 portions of the potato mixture into the
pan. Press down to flatten and round out to approximately 3 inches (7.5 cm) wide. You will need 8 flapjacks.

Cook the flapjacks on both sides until golden brown.

Remove from pan and reserve on absorbent paper.

Keep warm.

### Salmon Stack

Divide the herbed goat cheese into 4 portions and
slightly flatten into discs.

Mix together the mesclun lettuce, lemon rind, vinegar
and olive oil.

### Assembly

Place 1 flapjack on a serving plate. Top with a disc of
goat cheese.

Top the goat cheese with a 1/2 cup (125 mL) of the
lettuce. Top lettuce with 2 slices smoked salmon.
Complete with a second flapjack.

Garnish with a spoonful of whipped cream sprinkled
with chopped chives and caviar.

Finish remaining stacks in the same manner.

Serve immediately.

Ruth Benedikt
By The Way Café

By substituting Brie for a Mexican or Tex-Mex cheese, Ruth successfully creates a dish that is at once contemporary and traditional.

# Mediterranean Brie Quesadilla
## with Salsa Verde

5 small flour tortillas 5

1 lb Brie, rind removed 454 g

### Salsa Verde

½ tsp salt 2 mL

2 cloves garlic 10 g

½ lb tomatillos 227 g
husked, coarsely chopped

1 medium onion 200 g
chopped

3 serrano or jalapeño peppers 3
coarsely chopped

2 Tbsp fresh coriander 30 mL
chopped

1 ripe Haas avocado 1
halved, pit removed, diced

2 Tbsp olive oil 30 mL

**4 servings**

Preheat oven to 200°F (95°C).

In the bowl of a food processor fitted with the steel blade add the salt.

With the motor running, add the garlic and process it to paste consistency.

Add tomatillos, onion, chili or peppers and coriander. Process to a purée.

Place a saucepan over medium heat and add the purée. Cook for 5 minutes. Cool.

Add diced avocado to purée and pour into food processor. Process briefly just until avocado is blended into sauce.

Cover the surface of each tortilla with slices of Brie. Fold in half.

Place tortillas on cookie sheet and bake just until the cheese melts.

Cut each quesadilla into 3-4 wedges and serve warm with Salsa Verde spooned on top.

Ruth Benedikt
By The Way Café

"My husband, Amir, and I came together 20 years ago with very different perspectives about life. He comes from Israel and I was born in Mexico which combination, needless to say, represents a big cultural gap so it's no wonder we couldn't agree upon what constitutes 'good food.' Undaunted, we took over By The Way Café which we turned into a bistro café in 1986. We have brought together the best of our heritages, creating unusual combinations of Mediterranean and Latino dishes. After so many years and so much effort, we can proudly say that we are living proof that good food can bring two hearts together!"

# Mediterranean Grilled Vegetables
## in Veracruz Sauce

### Vegetables

1 large red pepper 200 g
  cut into thin strips

1 large yellow pepper 200 g
  cut into thin strips

1 large green pepper 200 g
  cut into thin strips

2 young zucchini 200 g
  cut into thin strips

medium eggplant 300 g
  peeled and cut into ¼-inch
  (.8-cm) strips

olive oil

### Veracruz Sauce

¼ cup extra virgin olive oil 80 mL

¼ cup fresh coriander 80 mL
  chopped

½ cup tomatoes 125 mL
  diced

1 tsp garlic 5 g
  minced

1 tsp Maggi seasoning 5 mL

2 tsp fresh lime juice 10 mL

to taste salt and pepper to taste

**4 servings**

Coat all the vegetables lightly with olive oil.

Heat a grill or grill pan over high heat.

Grill each vegetable separately, turning occasionally, until tender. Remove and place in a bowl. The eggplant may require additional oil and will take longer than the peppers and zucchini.

Combine all the sauce ingredients and mix well.

Toss with the grilled vegetables.

Serve at room temperature.

# salads, sides & vegetables

The Third Eat to the Beat found a new home in Toronto's circular concert venue, Roy Thomson Hall. In order to build revenues, we needed a location that could hold more chefs and more people comfortably. We wanted to eliminate many of the problems that had dogged the event, including excessive noise and line-ups.

It was a new challenge, indeed: we had to set up the space in just four hours. Tables, tableclothes, over 400 tea lights, set out and lit, silent auction, loot bags, grab bags, chef set-up, volunteer mobilization, VIP cocktail party all were ready to go when the doors opened at 6:30 PM.

With so much space, I figured that it would be great to set out the chefs the way one eats dinner: appetizers, soups, entrées and desserts one after the other. Boy, was I wrong! Everyone loved the food so much that no one wanted to miss a single table, so the lines were as long as ever even though we encouraged people to skip to less busy tables. And the dessert chefs (of whom I was one) stood idly by for about an hour before they were pounced upon by the eager hordes. I learned my lesson.

Salads, sides and vegetables are not usually conducive to this type of event so we don't get many chefs preparing them. However, they are an indispensable part of every chef's repertoire and there are some restaurants that specialize in them, and whose tables, perhaps because they alone feature them, are wildly popular.

This chapter provides you with full-meal salads, as well as some great vegetable dishes to serve for a grazing meal. Mom really was right; you must eat your vegetables, both for your health and to please her!

Bridget Lunn
Private Caterer

"My biggest challenge as a boardroom chef is to produce daily luncheon fare that is flavorful, nutritious and light. Main course salads are the perfect vehicle to exploit fruits and vegetables with their huge variety of colors and textures, which can so easily extend a small amount of calorie-rich protein."

# Avocado and Shaved Beet Salad

½ lemon 25 mL
  juiced

1 tsp fresh thyme 5 mL
  minced

1 ½ Tbsp champagne vinegar 20 mL

3 Tbsp extra-virgin olive oil 45 mL

to taste sea salt and freshly ground
  pepper to taste

pinch sugar pinch

4 small fresh beets 4
  washed and peeled

1 head Boston lettuce 1
  washed, dried and torn in half

2 small or 1 large Haas avocado
  2 small or 1 large

2 oz crumbled Stilton 55 g

½ lemon ½
  rind finely grated

**2 servings**

Whisk together lemon juice, thyme, vinegar, oil, salt, pepper and sugar. Taste and adjust seasoning.

Slice the beets paper thin with a mandoline and toss with 1 Tbsp (15 mL) dressing.

Toss some of the lettuce leaves with 1 Tbsp (15 mL) dressing and arrange on 2 plates.

Peel and pit the avocado. Slice into quarters.

Place avocado skin-side down among the lettuce leaves on each plate.

Place curls of beet between the avocado pieces.

Reserve the dressing that coated the beets and drizzle over the avocado.

Sprinkle salad with crumbled Stilton and lemon rind.

Serve immediately.

Kristen Aitken

Formely of The
Four Seasons Hotel

The Four Seasons has been a staunch supporter of Eat to the Beat, each year sending a different, but equally talented woman chef. It's thanks to the constant support of Meryl Witkin, the hotel's former marketing director, that the event gets such great coverage.

This is a fabulous salad. Don't be put off by the foie gras. If you can't find it or afford it or simply are daunted by it, substitute chicken livers for the classic French rendition. Lardons are thickly sliced pieces of bacon cut into small, thick pieces almost the size of croutons. Regular bacon may be substituted.

# Bitter Greens with Lardons, Mushrooms and Foie Gras

1 bunch arugula 1 bunch

1 head frisée lettuce 1 head

1 head radicchio 1 head

2 Belgian endives 2

1 Tbsp Dijon mustard 15 mL

3 Tbsp red wine vinegar 45 mL

½ cup olive oil 125 mL

2 shallots 2
    finely diced

to taste salt and pepper to taste

8 oz thick slice bacon 227g

3 Tbsp butter 45 g

20 cremini mushrooms 20
    bite-sized, cleaned and stemmed

8 oz foie gras 227g
    cut into 4 even slices

4 servings

Wash and dry all the lettuces and set aside.

To make the vinaigrette, place the mustard and red wine vinegar into a small bowl and whisk to blend.

Slowly add the olive oil and whisk to emulsify and thicken.

Add the shallots and taste for seasoning. Set aside.

Cut bacon crosswise into short 1/4-inch (.6-cm) strips.

In a small sauté pan, cook the bacon in 1 Tbsp butter until it has rendered almost all of its fat.

Drain on a paper towel and set aside.

In a medium sauté pan over medium heat, melt 1 Tbsp (15 mL) butter and add the mushrooms.

Cook until they begin to render their juices. Season with salt and pepper. Set aside but keep warm.

Toss the lettuces with the dressing and divide among 4 salad plates.

Heat a heavy-bottomed sauté pan over high heat and melt the remaining 1 Tbsp (15 mL) butter.

Add the foie gras and sear it very quickly (or else it will melt!) on each side.

Remove from the pan and place one slice on top of each salad.

Sprinkle the mushrooms and the bacon lardons evenly over each salad.

Serve immediately.

Esther Benaim &
Maggie McKeown
**Great Cooks &
The T Spot**

Great Cooks has a great space with a state-of-the-art kitchen on the lower level of the Hudson's Bay store on Queen Street in Toronto. There, Esther and Maggie provide cooking classes with many well-known chefs for anyone with an inclination for great food. This salad is an example of how you can spice up your winter repertoire without feeling in the least bit deprived of summer's abundance.

# Grilled Maple Pear and Pecan Salad

1 cup pecans 120 g

1 cup maple syrup 250 mL
   divided in half

2 pears 300 g
   just ripe, unpeeled, cored and sliced
   vertically

2 bunches fresh spinach 2 bunches
   washed, stemmed, and dried

½ cup white wine vinegar 125 mL

1 Tbsp Dijon mustard 15 mL

2 Tbsp lemon juice 30 mL

1½ cups vegetable oil 375 mL

to taste Parmesan cheese in a block
   to taste

salt and pepper

**6 servings**

Preheat oven to 350°F (180°C). Line a baking sheet with aluminum foil or Silpat.

Soak pecans in 1/2 cup (125 mL) maple syrup for 20 minutes.

In a separate bowl, marinate sliced pears in remaining 1/2 cup (125 mL) maple syrup.

Drain pecans and place on prepared cookie sheet. Bake for 20 minutes or until fork tender. Let cool before removing from cookie sheet.

Place spinach in a large mixing bowl.

Whisk together white wine vinegar and mustard. Gradually whisk in the oil to create an emulsion and thicken. Season with salt and pepper to taste. Set aside.

Heat grill or grill pan over high heat.

Drain the pears and quickly grill so that there are grill marks on one side. Remove and add to the bowl with the spinach.

Sprinkle the lemon juice over the salad.

Toss the salad with the dressing and divide among 6 plates.

Use a vegetable peeler to shave 3-4 Parmesan curls on top of salad.

Nettie Cronish

Cookbook Author /
Founder of Women's
Culinary Network

"As a cookbook author and cooking teacher, I meet people from all walks of life. And as a natural foods chef, I introduce these people to the benefits and delicious tastes of a vegetarian lifestyle. This recipe was well received at Eat to the Beat one year. For many people, it was the first time that they sampled tofu simply marinated in vinaigrette. Of course, the ingredients you use must be the best quality."

# Marinated Tofu Salad

## Marinade

¼ cup red wine vinegar 60 mL

3 Tbsp extra-virgin olive oil 45 mL

1 Tbsp lemon juice 15 mL

1 medium clove garlic 5 g
    minced

1 tsp salt 5 mL

½ tsp dried marjoram 3 mL

## Salad

8 oz firm tofu 227 g
    rinsed and cut into crouton-size
    pieces

4 asparagus stalks 4

1 cup broccoli florets 250 mL

1 carrot 130 g
    finely chopped

½ small red onion 100 g
    finely chopped

1 cup cooked chickpeas 250 mL

2 cups mixed greens 500 mL

**4-6 servings**

### Marinade

In a large bowl, whisk together all the ingredients.

### Salad

Place tofu in the bowl with the vinaigrette. Toss gently to coat and marinate 30 minutes.

Place a steamer basket or sieve in a pot of boiling water to use as a steamer.

Snap ends of asparagus off and steam until tender-crisp, about 4 minutes. (Keep steamer on the stove.)

Plunge asparagus into cold water to stop further cooking. Drain well and set aside.

Steam broccoli florets for about 4 minutes until tender-crisp.

Drain well. Add all vegetables and chickpeas to tofu and gently toss to coat. Marinate 1 hour.

Place mixed greens on platter and spoon tofu mixture on top.

Keeps up to 2 days, chilled.

Anne Donnelly
Chef
Arcadian Court

Thai cuisine loves the interplay of sour and sweet, salty and hot. It always amazes me how those combinations can work as well with chicken as with beef and yet still remain distinctly different. Despite the fact that there is beef in this recipe, it remains a very light dish.

# Thai Beef Salad

## Vinaigrette

1.5 oz lemon grass 45 g

3 oz fish sauce 85 mL

2 limes 15 mL
juiced

1 tsp serrano chilies 5 mL
minced

1 bunch mint leaves 56 g

5 heads garlic 227 g
peeled, chopped

2 cups honey 500 mL

1 cup vegetable oil 250 mL

## Salad

½ head radicchio 28 g
washed, dried

¼ head romaine 225 g
washed, dried

1 Belgian endive 1

½ English cucumber 50 g
thinly sliced

1 large whole tomato 275 g
sliced

½ red onion 100 g
thinly sliced

1 lb. sirloin steak 454 g

1 Tbsp + 1 tsp black pepper 20 mL

1 Tbsp + 1 tsp garlic 20 g
chopped

1 cup Thai dressing 250 mL

8 green onions 200 g
chopped

**4 servings**

### Vinaigrette

Remove outer leaves of lemon grass and place in food processor fitted with steel blade.

Add fish sauce, lime juice, minced chili with seeds, mint, garlic and honey.

Process until well blended. Gradually add oil and process until incorporated.

Refrigerate.

### Assembly

Divide bite-sized pieces of radicchio and romaine among 4 dinner plates. Arrange 3 endive leaves around the lettuce.

Arrange cucumbers around the lettuce and the tomatoes around the cucumbers. Distribute onions around the plates.

Refrigerate the plates while you prepare the steak.

Sprinkle the steak with black pepper and garlic.

Heat a heavy skillet until it is smoking. Add the steak and cook for 2 minutes on each side for rare.

Transfer to a cutting board and let stand 10 minutes before slicing.

Slice across the grain on the diagonal in very thin slices.

When ready to serve, toss the steak slices in a bowl with 1/4 cup (65 mL) of Vinaigrette.

Place a mound of beef on top of prepared plates and drizzle remaining dressing over all.

Garnish with chopped green onions.

Anne Donnelly
Chef
Arcadian Court

We always think that we know every woman chef in the city and yet Anne was completely unknown to us until one of our committee members, Randi Hampson, decided to get married and started to research venues. She and her mom, Sharon (of Sharon, Lois and Bram fame) settled on the Arcadian Court and introduced us to Anne. The rest is history. She has participated in Eat to the Beat ever since!

# Grilled Chicken and Vegetable Salad

## Vinaigrette

½ cup white wine vinegar 125 mL

1 Tbsp + 1 tsp Dijon mustard 20 mL

1 Tbsp + 1 tsp ground cumin 20 mL

1 cup olive oil 250 ml

2 tsp jalapeño pepper 10 mL
chopped

## Assembly

½ red onion 100 g

1 red pepper 200 g

4 small zucchini 480 g

1 can baby corn 225 g

¼ cup black olives 65 g
pitted

½ bunch parsley 56 g
stems removed

¼ cup vegetable oil 65 mL

4 chicken breasts 4
boneless, skinless

4 large Boston lettuce leaves 4

4 lemon slices 4

4 sprigs parsley 4

**4 servings**

## Vinaigrette

Combine vinegar, mustard, cumin, oil, and chopped jalapeño peppers.

Whisk together to blend.

## Assembly

Preheat grill or grill pan to high heat.

Finely chop onion and place in a medium bowl.

Cut pepper into quarters and clean out ribs and seeds. Cut into thin strips and add to bowl.

Cut zucchini in half lengthwise and brush with olive oil. Grill zucchini 1 minute on each side. Slice into 6 pieces on the diagonal. Cool. When completely cool, add to the vegetables in the bowl.

Drain corn and olives and add to the vegetables. Add parsley and toss the vegetables together.

Toss vegetables with half the dressing.

Brush chicken breasts with vegetable oil on all sides. Place on hot grill for 7-9 minutes, turning once.

Remove to a cutting board. Let cool about 5 minutes.

Slice into 5-6 pieces each on the diagonal.

On each of 4 serving plates, place 1 lettuce leaf.

Spoon 1 cup (250 mL) of vegetables into the center of the lettuce.

Fan 5-6 chicken slices in front of the vegetables but on top of the lettuce.

Drizzle each plate with remaining dressing.

Garnish with lemon slices and parsley.

Joan Monfaredi

Executive Chef
Park Hyatt Hotel

"The idea for this salad came from frustration over the ongoing requests for club sandwiches. If people like club sandwiches so much, we reasoned, surely they will like a club salad. Indeed, they do! I have had this item on our menu for more than five years and it continues to be a top seller. It contains all the good and recognizable ingredients of a club sandwich but is happily consumed with a knife and fork."

# Club House Salad

### Creamy Herb Dressing

2 cups mayonnaise 500 mL

4 Tbsp fresh lemon juice 45 mL

2 Tbsp fresh herbs 30 mL
chopped (thyme, parsley, chives,etc.)

to taste salt and pepper to taste

### Club Salad

3 Tbsp Creamy Herb Dressing 45 g

2 leaves red leaf lettuce 2 leaves
pulled into pieces

2 slices aged cheddar 30 g

1, 6 oz. chicken breast 165 g
cooked, boneless, skinless

2 slices beefsteak tomato 2 slices

2 slices crisp, cooked bacon 40 g

2 bagel crisps 2

1 serving

Toss the lettuce with a little of the dressing and place on a plate.

Layer the cheddar, chicken and tomato on top.

Drizzle with more dressing.

Artfully place the bacon strips and bagel crisps.

Serve immediately.

Anne Donnelly
Chef
Arcadian Court

As soon as Thai food hit the Toronto scene, versions of this salad were everywhere. This one is particularly good what with its combination of lush mango and peanut butter contrasted with sharp lime juice and salty fish sauce.

Give it a try. You won't ever go back to your everyday chicken salad again!

# Chicken and Mango Salad

## Dressing

2 lbs green mango 1 kg
 peeled

8 oz red and green peppers 225 g
 sliced into thin strips

1 tsp salt 5 g

3 limes 30 mL
 juiced

3 oz vegetable oil 85 mL

4 Tbsp garlic 60 g
 chopped

2 bunches green onion 200 g
 sliced

1/3 cup fish sauce 85 mL

1/3 cup crunchy peanut butter 85 g

1/4 cup + 2 Tbsp brown sugar 85 g

1/2 tsp black pepper 2 mL
 ground

1/4 cup serrano chili 30 g
 seeded diced finely chopped

1/2 red onion 100 g

## Assembly

4 pieces leaf lettuce 4 pieces

mango salad

4 8-oz chicken breasts 225 g
 poached*, minced

1 Tbsp fresh coriander 15 mL
 chopped

1 Tsp crushed chilies 5 mL

**4 servings**

### Dressing

Cut mango into julienne strips and place in a large bowl. Add thin strips of green and red pepper. Sprinkle with salt and lime juice.

Heat vegetable oil in a medium frying pan. Add garlic and green onions. Cook until garlic is softened.

Lower heat and add fish sauce, peanut butter, sugar, pepper and chili peppers. Cook until peanut butter has melted. Stir well and remove from heat.

Pour over mangos and peppers in bowl. Add red onions and mix thoroughly.

Chill thoroughly.

### Assembly

Place 1 lettuce leaf on the side of each of 4 dinner plates. Fill the other side with mango salad, slightly overlapping the lettuce leaf.

Top salad with chicken. Sprinkle each plate with finely chopped coriander and crushed chilies.

Serve immediately.

### *To poach chicken breasts

Remove any loose bits of breast, like the filet. Place the chicken breasts and filets in a medium saucepan. Cover with cold water.

Place over medium heat and bring to a gentle simmer. Simmer for 10-15 minutes, depending upon the thickness of the breasts.

Turn off heat and let sit in hot water for an additional 10 minutes. Remove. Cool.

Mary Ellen Elliott

Jason Rosso was inspired to become a chef by his grand-mother Mary Ellen Elliott. He became an enthusiastic supporter of Eat to the Beat as soon as he arrived at Peller Estates, sending a team of talented young women to the event.

# Lentil and Roasted Garlic Salad
## with Smoked Bacon Vinaigrette

### Salad

1 lb green French lentils (du Puy) 454 g

1 medium red onion 200 g
  finely diced

1 medium tomato 250 g
  seeded and diced

10 cloves roasted garlic whole 50 g

3 Tbsp sun-dried tomatoes 45 mL
  finely chopped

### Vinaigrette

6 slices thick cut bacon 6 slices
  coarsely chopped

1 cup grape seed oil 250 mL

½ cup red wine vinegar 125 mL

splash balsamic vinegar splash

2 Tbsp chopped fresh herbs
  parsley, dill, thyme, etc. 30 mL

to taste salt and pepper to taste

**6 good-size appetizer or
lunch salads**

### Salad

Cook the lentils in unsalted water until soft, about 30 minutes. Drain and let cool.

Add remaining ingredients and toss gently.

Make the vinaigrette.

### Vinaigrette

Fry the coarsely chopped bacon until crisp. Drain on a paper towel reserving one third of the bacon fat.

Place bacon in a stainless steel bowl with one third of the bacon fat as well.

Add the rest of the dressing ingredients and whisk together. Season to taste.

### Assembly

Place the lentil salad in a large sauté pan.

Add as much of the vinaigrette as you like.

Gently warm and serve.

### Editor's Note

This salad must be served slightly warm because of the bacon fat in the vinaigrette.

Wendy Hernick
**Sage Café and Catering**

"This salad is so popular that our customers actually get upset when we don't make it!"

# Roasted Potato Salad

4 medium potatoes 800 g

2 medium sweet potatoes 500 g

to taste salt and pepper to taste

1 clove garlic 5 g
   minced

2 sprigs rosemary 2 sprigs
   broken into pieces

3 Tbsp olive oil 45 mL

¾ cup green onion 50 g
   chopped

1 cup celery 120 g
   diced

½ cup green pepper 60 g
   diced

½ cup red pepper 60 g
   diced

2 cups cucumber 200 g
   diced

### Vinaigrette

4 Tbsp Dijon mustard 60 mL

½ cup red wine vinegar 125 mL

½ tsp garlic 2 mL
   chopped

1 Tbsp sugar 15 mL

¾ cup vegetable oil 185 mL

¾ cup olive oil 185 mL

to taste salt and pepper to taste

**6 servings**

Preheat oven to 375°F (190°C).

Peel and cut potatoes into wedges, about 6-8 per potato.

Place them in a bowl and season with salt and pepper, rosemary, garlic, and olive oil.

Place in roasting pan and bake for up to 1 hour or until fork tender.

Cool potatoes until they are just warm and add all the other salad ingredients.

Add the Vinaigrette and toss together to coat well.

Best served on the same day.


Vinaigrette

Whisk mustard, vinegar, garlic and sugar together in a small bowl.

Slowly add the vegetable oil, whisking constantly.

Continue to whisk in the olive oil. The dressing should be thick and creamy.

Season with salt and pepper to taste.

Wendy Blackwood

Loblaws Cooking
Schools

"For the past ten years, as an avid gardener, I have been growing a variety of fruits and vegetables in my downtown Toronto backyard and at my house near Kingston. In town, my garden boasts golden raspberries, blackberries, cherry, and apple trees. And in the summer there is an ever-increasing selection of heirloom tomatoes and potatoes.

Potatoes are my true love and my garden has included German fingers, pink/gold skinned Desirée, purple skin longlac, the trendy all-blues, and short-lived all reds—all of which have participated in the search for the perfect gratin!"

# Swiss Chard and Potato Gratin

1 lb Swiss chard 454 g
red, green or rainbow

2 large cloves garlic 20 g

2 shallots 30 g
finely chopped

2 tsp olive oil 10 mL

1 tsp fresh thyme leaves 5 mL
finely chopped or
½ tsp (2 mL) dried

3 lbs potatoes* 1.5 kg
peeled and thinly sliced

8 oz aged Gouda cheese 227 g
shredded

to taste salt and pepper to taste

1 cup fresh breadcrumbs 130 g

6 servings

Preheat oven to 375°F (190°C).

Wash chard and cut off toughest bottom part of stems.

Place the chard in a large pot with about 1 cup (250 mL) water and bring to a boil.

Cover and steam until the stems are soft and the leaves are wilted, about 5 minutes.

Cool and squeeze out as much moisture as possible. Chop roughly.

In a large frying pan set over low/medium heat, sauté the garlic and shallots in olive oil until translucent.

Add thyme and chard and cook gently until all the excess water has evaporated. Do not brown.

Oil a 4-6 cup (1 L-1.5 L) gratin dish. Layer one third of the potato slices in the bottom, season with salt and pepper and cover with one third of the shredded cheese.

Repeat a layer of potatoes, season and cover with Swiss chard and a layer of cheese.

Cover with a final layer of potatoes and the rest of the cheese.

Bake uncovered for 40 minutes. Remove and cover with breadcrumbs.

Return to the oven and bake for 15 minutes. Serve immediately.

# chapter 4

# soups

Somehow, Eat to the Beat had survived into its fourth year. None of us on the founding committee could quite believe that the time had passed so quickly. We felt confident about the coming event, but each year brought new surprises, so the pre-event anxiety paralleled our excitement.

This year, it was a dark and stormy night. Eat to the Beat had been pushed into the beginning of November, competing with a number of other high-visibility charitable events. The rain lashed against the windows of Roy Thomson Hall, and people hardy enough to defy the elements scurried for shelter in the face of heavy winds and biting rain.

We wrestled with finding the right balance of guests to guest experience, accessibility to people of most income levels and the reality of Willow's financial needs, as well as making the event interesting enough year after year to continue to draw widespread community support. After all, every guest who attended could spread the word about Willow's services.

This was the year that we invited interior designers to create magical spaces, every item in which was part of our silent auction. The rooms alone, elegant, glamorous and glittering, raised $20,000 for Willow. We were thrilled with the results.

We had learned a lot. For example, if we had a sell-out year with 800 guests, it was great for fundraising but not so great for the guests. Word of mouth had it that the food was superb, but the waits were not. Almost invariably, the following year saw fewer guests who had a sensational time and raved about Eat to the Beat, resulting in record numbers the next year … and so the cycle continued. Every year we debate cutting the number of tickets and raising the price or keeping the ticket price and finding a larger venue to accommodate more guests. We want to provide a gratifying event for the guests and the chefs as well as the greatest possible proceeds for Willow.

When you are confronted with a dark and stormy night, turn to soup. A well-prepared soup represents comfort, no matter how lowly or sophisticated it may be. Slowly, as soups entered the repertoire of Eat to the Beat, many chefs recognized their ease of pre-event preparation and service. Some of the soups in this chapter are quick to put together while others require some finer ingredients and more time. Each, though, reflects the chef's quirky approach to some of the most basic ingredients.

Whether you decide to make them from beginning to end or just jump in and choose one from the middle, you will be glad you did.

Wendy Hernick
**Sage Café and Catering**

"There is nothing better than a bowl of this delicious soup on a chilly day. Large pots of it seem to walk out the door when it is on the menu!"

# Roasted Potato Soup

2 medium PEI potatoes 400 g
  peeled, cubed

1 medium sweet potato 250 g

2 medium parsnips 200 g
  peeled, cubed

1 medium carrot 100 g
  peeled, cubed

1 small butternut squash 400 g
  peeled, cubed

¼ cup olive oil 65 mL

generous pinch each thyme, basil,
  oregano generous pinch each

1 Tbsp olive oil 15 mL

1 large onion 250 g
  diced

2 cloves garlic 10 g
  minced

2 quarts water, vegetable or chicken
  stock 2 L

to taste salt and pepper to taste

**6 servings**

Preheat oven to 400°F (200°C).

Toss all the vegetables together in a large bowl.

Add 1/4 cup (65 mL) olive oil and coat well.

Season with salt and pepper.

Add herbs and toss again.

Place in a roasting pan and bake for 30 minutes or until vegetables are almost done.

Drain off any excess oil.

In a stockpot, heat the 1 Tbsp (15 mL) oil over medium heat.

Add the onion and garlic and sweat until transparent and soft.

Add the roast vegetables and toss.

Add enough water or stock to cover.

Simmer for 20-30 minutes until the vegetables are very soft.

Purée in the bowl of a food processor fitted with the steel blade until it is thick but not the texture of baby food!

Taste and season with salt and pepper if needed.

You may serve the soup immediately but it freezes well, too and improves if made a day or two prior to serving.

Izabela Kalabis
Chef
Inniskillin Wines

"Apart from the obvious love of food in its purest form, it took me a while to realize that it is the adrenalin rush I experience when cooking that thrills me. I won't ever forget serving this chowder at the most recent Eat to the Beat. My friend Judy attempted to transfer a huge Le Creuset pot (i.e. extremely heavy) of hot chowder from burner to table. Well, her hands 'just did not work at that moment' as she put it and the pot of very hot chowder went flying into our eyes, hair, faces, clothes, before finally landing on the floor. Luckily, nobody got badly burned and I had tons of chowder. We were trying to wash chowder from our eyes as elegant guests arrived!"

# Jerusalem Artichoke and Yukon Gold Chowder
## with Sautéed Wild Mushrooms and Goat Cheese Croutes

4 Tbsp butter 56 g

1 medium onion 200 g
chopped

2 cloves garlic 10 g
minced

2 parsnips 150 g
peeled and chopped

½ lb Yukon gold potatoes 250 g
peeled, chopped

2 lbs Jerusalem artichokes 1 kg
peeled and chopped

4 cups chicken or vegetable stock 1 L

2 cups mushroom stock 500 mL

½ cup 35% whipping cream 125 mL

pinch freshly grated nutmeg pinch

to taste salt and pepper to taste

### Garnish

1 cup mixed wild mushrooms 250 g
cleaned and chopped

1 Tbsp butter 15 g

1 clove garlic 5 g
minced

1 Tbsp parsley 15 mL
minced

to taste sea salt, freshly ground
black pepper to taste

8 small rounds sourdough bread
8 small rounds

2½ oz goat cheese 75 g

**8 servings**

Melt butter over medium heat in a large pot. Add onions and sweat until soft and translucent.

Add garlic. Cook for 1 minute before adding parsnips, potatoes, and Jerusalem artichokes. Cook for 1 minute.

Add stocks, season, and bring to a simmer.

Cook soup until vegetables are tender, about 30 minutes.

When cooked, purée and add cream and nutmeg, adjusting the seasoning to taste.

For the garnish, sauté the mushrooms in butter and add the garlic, salt and pepper and cook until just releasing their liquid. Remove from the heat.

Toast bread rounds until lightly golden.

Place a bit of goat cheese on top of each round and place under the broiler, just until the cheese begins to melt.

Serve soup hot, sprinkled with parsley and mushrooms with 1 croute per person.

Lisa Slater

Co-Founder
Eat to the Beat /
Whole Foods
Market

Shabin is a neighbor of mine who moved from Vancouver to Toronto. She invited me in for lunch one dreary, cold autumn day. The house smelled wonderful: exotic and warm. Shabin was making this soup, which the two of us consumed completely, bowl after bowl.

Shabin explained to me that this is one of those dishes that people from the Indian subcontinent, Indians as well as Pakistanis, cook without a specific recipe, making individual, signature versions. So you can spice it up or tone it down, make it more or less tart to suit your own preferences. But whatever you do, don't forget the salt which brings out the flavor of the combined ingredients.

# Shabin's Chana e Batata Soup

2 Yukon gold potatoes 500 g
   peeled and cut into ¼-inch
   (.8-cm) cubes

1 Tbsp vegetable oil 15 mL

1 tsp turmeric 5 mL

1 15-oz can cooked chickpeas 420 mL
   drained

3-4 cups water 750 mL – 1 L

pinch cayenne pepper pinch

1-2 lemons 1-2
   juiced

to taste salt to taste

1 Tbsp cilantro 15 mL
   minced

**2 servings**

Heat the oil in a large saucepan and add the potatoes.

Add the turmeric and toss to coat.

Cook over moderate heat for about 4 minutes.

Add the chickpeas and enough water to cover by 1/2 inch (1.2 cm).

Bring to a boil and reduce to a simmer.

Cook until the potatoes are fork tender but not mushy.

Add the cayenne pepper.

Add lemon juice and salt. Taste. Adjust so that there is a nice balance between salty and tangy.

Add the cilantro and stir to blend.

Serve immediately.

Claire Stubbs

Mildred Pierce
Restaurant

Claire is known for her inventive cooking style. She is a traveler who picks up ideas and inspirations from the places she visits and the cuisine she discovers along the way. This is a lush soup made rich by a fresh corn stock and coconut milk. It is a must-try.

# Indian-Style White Corn Soup

### Corn Stock

10 peaches and cream corn cobs 10

2 onions 400 g
  peeled and chopped

4 cloves garlic 20 g
  crushed

2 carrots 200 g
  peeled and chopped

3 celery stalks 180 g
  cut into 2-inch (5-cm) pieces

1 bay leaf 1

1 tsp whole black peppercorns 5 mL

### Soup Base

¼ cup butter 65 g

1 Tbsp garlic 15 g
  finely chopped

1 cup Vidalia onions 125 g
  chopped

2 tsp curry paste 10 mL

1 yellow pepper 200 g
  roasted

5 cups fresh corn kernels 800 g

6 cups corn stock 1.5 L

1 can coconut milk 300 mL

1 Tbsp kosher salt 21 g

½ tsp sambal 2 mL

2 Tbsp cilantro 30 mL
  finely chopped

12 mini pappadams 12
  fried

**8 servings**

### Corn Stock

Cut the corn niblets from the cobs. Set corn aside and place the cobs in a large stockpot.

Add the onions, garlic, carrots, celery, bay leaf and peppercorns to the pot. Fill with enough cold water to just cover the ingredients.

Bring to a boil and simmer for 1 hour.

Strain the liquid through a fine strainer into a bowl and set aside.

### Soup Base

Melt the butter in a large pot. Add the garlic and the Vidalia onions and sauté for 5 minutes until soft but not brown.

Stir in the curry paste, roasted yellow pepper, and fresh corn kernels. Cook over medium low heat for 10 minutes, stirring occasionally.

Pour in the corn stock and simmer gently for 40 minutes.

Add the coconut milk and heat through.

Purée the soup in batches in a food processor or blender.

Pass the soup through a fine strainer for a silky texture.

Pour the soup into bowls. Season with the kosher salt and sambal.

Garnish each portion with cilantro and mini pappadams.

### Editor's Note

Curry paste and sambal can be found in the ethnic section of most supermarkets. The sambal may be omitted if less heat is preferred.

Suzanne Baby

**Gallery Grill at
Hart House**

I love it when chefs take a lowly item like celeriac and pair it with something high-brow like oysters, elevating the former and rendering the latter approachable, all in a single dish. Imagine doing that all within something as comforting as this soup ....

# Celeriac and Potato Soup
## with Poached Oysters and Caviar Whipped Crème Fraiche

¼ cup unsalted butter 65 g

1 cup leeks 120 g
  finely sliced

½ cup dry white wine 125 mL

4 cups chicken or fish stock 1 L

½ cup potatoes 50 g
  peeled, slivered

½ cup celeriac 50 g
  peeled, slivered

¼-½ cup 35% whipping cream
  60-125 mL (optional)

to taste salt and pepper to taste

24 fresh oysters 24
  to taste

4-8 Tbsp crème fraiche 60-125 mL

4 Tbsp caviar 60 mL

2 Tbsp chives 30 mL
  chopped


**4 servings**

Place butter into a medium saucepan and add the leeks. Over low heat, sweat the leeks until very soft.

Deglaze the pan by pouring the white wine over the leeks.

Add the stock, potatoes, and celeriac. Simmer until potatoes and celeriac are tender.

Either using an immersion blender or a food processor, purée the soup.

Add cream if using and return to the heat. Season to taste.

Shuck oysters, reserving their liquor (juice).

Pour the oyster liquor through a fine sieve into a small saucepan.

Add the oysters and over low heat poach them for a few seconds on each side. Remove from the heat.

Fold the caviar into crème fraiche.

Place the oysters into 4 small, warm serving bowls. Evenly pour the soup over the oysters.

Divide the caviar and sprinkle the chopped chives over each of the soups.

Mary Bourke

**Blue Agave
Caters to You**

Mary Bourke specializes in Southwestern comfort food. She and her son operate a restaurant down on Queen Street that has found a nifty niche for itself catering to corporate clients and people who want to take over an entire restaurant. Mary is pleased to oblige and serves great food.

# Mom's Spicy Vegetable and Chickpea Soup

3 Tbsp extra virgin olive oil 45 mL

1 large onion 250 g
   diced

1 ½ Tbsp minced garlic 20 g

3 carrots 300 g
   diced

1 green pepper 200 g
   cored, seeded, diced

1 red pepper 200 g
   cored, seeded, diced

1 orange pepper 200 g
   cored, seeded, diced

2 medium zucchini 240 g
   diced

2 stalks celery 150 g
   diced

1, 28-oz can plum tomatoes 784 mL

2 Tbsp tomato paste 30 mL

6-7 cups vegetable stock 1.5-1.75 L

1 ½ cups fresh or frozen corn 245 g

1, 18-oz canned chickpeas 500 g
   drained

2 tsp ground cumin 10 mL

1 Tbsp fresh thyme 15 mL
   chopped

2 tsp chili powder 10 mL

½-1 tsp chili flakes 2-5 mL
   to taste

to taste salt and pepper to taste

garnish roughly crumbled nacho chips

optional toppings grated cheddar,
   sour cream, salsa, fresh cilantro

**6 servings**

In a stock pot, heat the olive oil over medium heat until very hot.

Add the onion and garlic and sauté for about 3 minutes, stirring to coat with oil.

Add carrots, peppers, zucchini, and celery and sauté an additional 3 minutes.

Add the tomatoes, stir, and then add the tomato paste, and stir again.

Add the vegetable stock, corn, chickpeas and spices.

Reduce the heat and simmer for 1 hour or until the vegetables are tender. Add more stock if you want a more liquid soup.

Ladle into bowls and garnish with optional garnishes and nacho chips.

Jan Sherk
**Word of Mouth
Cuisine**

When you think about it, gazpacho and shrimp seem like a match made in heaven. Not only is the combination visually beautiful, but the flavors complement one another in a dish that could easily be served as an appetizer or a full meal accompanied by some hot, crusty bread and some crisp, white wine.

# Gazpacho with Grilled Shrimp

3 large ripe tomatoes 1 kg

1 small onion 150 g

1 clove garlic 5 g

1 English cucumber 100 g
    seeded

1 small jalapeño pepper 1
    seeded

1 ¾ cups tomato juice 450 mL

¼ cup white wine vinegar 65 mL

2 tsp extra virgin olive oil 10 mL

½ cup dry white wine 125 mL

1 tsp paprika 5 mL

½ tsp salt 2 mL

2 dashes cumin 2 dashes

dash hot sauce dash

dash Worcestershire sauce dash

### Garnishes

18 large shrimp 18
    peeled, deveined

¼ cup extra virgin olive oil 65 mL

to taste salt and pepper to taste

½ avocado ½
    diced

¼ yellow pepper 50 g
    diced

¼ red pepper 50 g
    diced

½ cup croutons 75 g
    toasted

¼ bunch chives ¼ bunch
    cut in 1-inch (2.5-cm) lengths

Coarsely chop tomatoes, onion, garlic, cucumber, and jalapeño pepper.

Place in a large bowl, pour tomato juice over and mix.

Let stand 2 hours at room temperature.

Add the remaining ingredients except the garnishes.

Process in batches, blend until smooth and strain through a sieve.

Chill overnight.

Chill serving bowls.

Toss shrimp with olive oil, salt and pepper.

Grill on both sides until just cooked.

Pour soup into serving bowls, top with garnishes and 3 grilled shrimp apiece.

Top with chives.

**6 servings**

Suzanne Baby
Gallery Grill at
Hart House

Suzanne can always be counted on to provide an element of surprise in her cooking. Consider the chickpeas as croutons, perhaps not as crisp but providing just enough texture and spiciness as a counterpoint to the fairly mellow eggplant. When was the last time you made a soup with eggplant? Now's definitely the time!

# Charred Eggplant Soup
## with Spiced Chickpeas

4 medium, firm eggplants 1.2 kg

¼ cup olive oil 65 mL

1 large onion 250 g
   diced

3 Tbsp garlic 45 g
   finely chopped

1 cup dry white wine 250 mL

6 cups chicken stock (or water) 1 L

to taste salt and pepper to taste

¼ cup extra virgin olive oil 65 mL

2 Tbsp fresh lemon juice 30 mL

### Spiced Chickpeas

¼ cup cooked chickpeas 75 g

1 Tbsp finely chopped red onions 15 g

½ tsp ground coriander 2 mL

pinch ground turmeric pinch

½ tsp ground anise seed 2 mL

pinch ground fennel seed pinch

pinch chili flakes pinch

1 ½ inches fresh ginger 3.8 cm
   peeled, finely grated

1 Tbsp extra virgin olive oil 15 mL

1 Tbsp fresh lemon juice 15 mL

1 Tbsp fresh coriander 15 mL
   chopped

to taste salt and pepper to taste

6 servings

Over an open flame or under the broiler, char the skin of the eggplant until the flesh is completely soft and skins are blackened and brittle. Set aside until cool enough to peel. Peel and discard the skin.

In a large saucepan, sauté the onions until soft in olive oil. Add garlic and sauté 1 minute.

Add the wine, stock, or water, and eggplant.

Simmer over low to medium heat for 20-30 minutes.

Using an immersion blender or food processor, purée the soup.

Strain through a medium sieve. Season to taste with salt and pepper.

Keep warm over very low heat.

When ready to serve, pour in extra virgin olive oil and lemon juice.

Spiced Chickpeas

Toss all the ingredients together. Taste for seasoning.

To serve, ladle soup into soup bowls. Spoon chickpeas into the center of each bowl.

Lynn Mendelson
Caterer

"I am a busy Toronto caterer and mother of four children. I am the sole proprietor of the aptly named Lynn Mendelson Catering and author of *Chicken! Chicken! Chicken!* and *Chicken! Chicken and More Chicken!*

"I get my inspiration from my mother, Roz, also a mother of four and late entry into the work force. My mother is an excellent cook, but unfortunately limited in scope, so I get my recipes from my sister Susan Mendelson of The Lazy Gourmet in Vancouver. When I am not overeating, I am taking advice from my other sister Rena Mendelson and sharing laughter with my brother Fred."

# Mulligatawny Soup

1 white onion 250 g, quartered

2 carrots 200 g, peeled, quartered

2 stalks celery 150 g, quartered

1 leek 75 g, white only, washed
   cut into 1-inch (2.5-cm) pieces

1 small tart apple 150 g
   peeled, cored, quartered

2 Tbsp vegetable oil 30 mL

2 Tbsp unsalted butter 30 g

3 sprigs fresh parsley 3 sprigs, chopped

2 cloves garlic 10 g, minced

1 tsp fresh ginger 5 mL, peeled, minced

2 tsp curry powder 10 mL

2 tsp ground cumin 10 mL

1 Tbsp ground coriander 15 mL

pinch each of mustard seed, chili powder,
   ground cloves, ground mace
   pinch each of

4 ½ cups chicken stock 1.1 L

1 bay leaf 1

to taste salt and pepper to taste

2 whole chicken breasts 450 g
   skinless, boneless, cut into 1-inch
   x ¼-inch (2.5-cm x .6 cm) strips

½ cup rice 100 g

1 Tbsp tomato paste 15 mL

1 firm, ripe tomato 250 g
   peeled, seeded, chopped

3 Tbsp fresh lemon juice 45 mL

2 Tbsp fresh cilantro 30 mL, chopped

2 limes cut in wedges

In the bowl of a food processor fitted with the steel blade, process the onion, carrots, celery, leek, and apple until minced.

In a large pot set over medium heat, melt the butter and oil and add the minced vegetables.

Sauté until caramelized and golden brown.

Stir in all the herbs and spices, chicken stock and bay leaf. Stir to blend.

Bring to a boil. Reduce the heat to low, cover, and simmer for 25 minutes.

Season to taste with salt and pepper.

Add the chicken pieces, rice, tomato paste, tomato, and lemon juice to the soup.

Simmer for 5-10 minutes, stirring occasionally until chicken is cooked through.

Ladle into bowls and garnish with chopped cilantro.

Serve with lime wedges on the side.

**6-8 servings**

Kristen Aitken

Formerly of The
Four Seasons Hotel

This is an example of the elegant yet simple cooking going on at the Four Seasons Café these days. You don't have to be rich and famous to be able to enjoy the surroundings and the food because it is all meant to be inviting. Now, with this recipe, you can have it all at home, too.

# Wild Mushroom Bisque
## with Garlic Asiago Croutons

### Mushroom Soup

2 Tbsp butter 30 g

2 Tbsp olive oil 30 mL

1 large onion 250 g
  diced

1 clove garlic 1
  diced

2 shallots 30 g
  diced

1 pound assorted fresh mushrooms
  454 g roughly chopped

1 bay leaf 1

2 sprigs fresh thyme 2

½ cup white wine 125 mL

1 quart chicken stock 1 L

to taste salt and pepper to taste

1 lemon 45 mL
  juiced

to drizzle Basil Oil (recipe follows)

### Mushroom Soup

In a large heavy-bottomed saucepan, melt the butter with the oil over medium heat.

Add the onion, garlic, and shallots and sweat them until they are translucent, about 5 minutes.

Add the mushrooms, bay leaf and thyme, cooking and stirring until most of the liquid from the mushrooms has evaporated.

Deglaze the pan by adding the white wine and allow to cook until it is almost completely dry.

Add the chicken stock and bring to to a simmer. Cook for 20 minutes.

Use an immersion blender, a food processor or an upright blender to purée the soup until it is very smooth.

Pass the soup through a fine mesh strainer and return to the pot. Adjust the seasoning and add the lemon juice to bring out the flavor.

### Garlic Asiago Croutons

1 clove garlic 5 g
  finely chopped

2 Tbsp extra virgin olive oil 30 mL

1 baguette 1
  sliced on the diagonal into ½ inch
  (1.2 cm) pieces

3 oz Asiago cheese 85 g
  grated

1 bunch chives 1
  finely chopped

### Garlic Asiago Croutons

Mix the garlic with the olive oil and brush onto one side of each bread slice.

Place on a cookie sheet.

Sprinkle the Asiago evenly over the pieces.

Place under the broiler until the cheese is bubbly.

Sprinkle with the chopped chives.

## Basil Oil

1 cup extra virgin olive oil 250 mL

½ bunch fresh basil ½ bunch
   leaves plucked off, washed and
   dried, coarsely chopped

**4 servings**

### Basil Oil

Place olive oil in a small saucepan. Over very low heat warm the oil just until you can smell its fragrance.

Remove the pan from the heat and add the basil leaves. Allow to steep for a few hours.

Store in the fridge. It will become cloudy but return to its liquid state at room temperature. Strain before using.

### Assembly

Pour the soup into 4 bowls and drizzle with Basil Oil.

Garnish with a crouton placed diagonally across the top of the soup bowl, if it is small enough. If it is a large bowl, float the crouton right on the soup.

# chapter 5

# entrées

Year Five. There was great excitement this year. It was, after all, the millennium year. We had to compete with upcoming year-end festivities and still bring Willow its sorely needed income. What would interest people enough to choose Eat to the Beat over other meaningful fundraisers—in other words, how could we beat the competition?

We introduced Niagara wineries and Ontario microbreweries to sample alongside the food; we had designer dinner tables dressed to the nines; we introduced our now famous Meal Ticket which entitled the highest bidder to 12 meals for two at Toronto's most glamorous restaurants, and we had the Champagne Diamond Draw.

Guests would pay $100 to purchase a numbered champagne flute. There would be a draw for a beautiful diamond ring. It seemed so simple. The reality was far from it: from figuring out how to attach the numbers to the champagne flutes and keeping duplicates of them, to getting guests to part with $100 a shot, we were sweating bullets the entire evening. In the end, we reduced the price to $75 a ticket, and (luckily) we sold out. Someone did indeed go home with a diamond ring worth over $2000. We swore we would never try *that* again!

The recipes in this chapter will not make you sweat bullets nor swear never to do them again. Instead, you will want to do them all, again and again. Most of the recipes are straightforward; some have an abundance of ingredients, but take heart, since the techniques are easy. There are recipes you can use every day and serve to guests with great results. None is fussy and all are rich with flavour and variety.

Liza Hardoon

To Go
Savoury & Thyme
Catering

Liza caters in people's homes and offers great takeout dishes for those of us who simply don't have the time or inclination to cook. She understands the need to provide things that people might make themselves without being too fancy or fussy. Don't miss the step of reducing the sauce that marks the difference between a good and a great chef and a good and a great dish. The flavors concentrate, the sauce thickens, and the dish becomes a classic.

# Zinfandel of Beef

4 lbs boneless beef stew meat 2 kg
cut into 2-inch (5-cm) cubes

2-4 Tbsp vegetable oil 30-60 mL
as needed

2 cups cipollini onions 100 g
peeled

1 cup carrots 150 g
cut in small dice

2 cups cremini mushrooms 200 g

4 cups Zinfandel wine 1 L

3 cups beef stock 750 mL

3 large cloves garlic 25 g
unpeeled

2 cups canned tomatoes 500 mL
drained, crushed

1 bay leaf 1

1 tsp thyme 5 mL

to taste salt and pepper to taste

**8-9 servings**

Preheat oven to 350°F (180°C).

Dry the meat thoroughly with a paper towel.

Cover the bottom of a large, heavy frying pan with a fine film of vegetable oil and set over medium high heat.

When the pan and the oil get very hot, brown the beef cubes in small batches being sure not to crowd the beef or else it will steam instead of browning. Turn the meat frequently so that it browns on all sides, 3-5 minutes. As it cooks, transfer the meat to a 3-quart (3-L) heavy casserole dish.

Remove all but 1 Tbsp (15mL) of fat from the frying pan. Add the vegetables, and stir often until they begin to brown. Remove and place them over the beef in the casserole.

Deglaze the pan by pouring 1 cup (250 mL) of wine into the frying pan. Stir to blend the juices and to dislodge any crispy bits sticking to the bottom. Bring to a simmer and pour over the beef and vegetables.

To the casserole, add the garlic, 3 cups (750 mL) of wine, 2 cups (500 mL) of beef stock, tomatoes, bay leaf, thyme, and salt to taste.

Bring to a simmer. Cover and place in the oven for 2-1/2 to 3 hours or until the stew meat is fork tender. Check from time to time to see if there is enough liquid. If it seems to be drying out, add some or all of the remaining beef stock.

When done, remove from the oven and strain the beef into a colander set over a saucepan. Press out the juices.

Set the saucepan over medium high heat and bring to a boil. Boil down rapidly for 5 minutes.

Transfer the meat to a serving dish and pour the thickened sauce over the meat.

Mary Bourke

**Blue Agave
Caters to You**

This is an example of Mary's no-fuss, no-nonsense cooking that nonetheless delivers great taste and texture.

# Mom's Southwestern Pot Roast

1 tsp ground cumin 5 mL

3 Tbsp chili powder 45 mL

1 tsp kosher salt 5 mL

3 lb cross rib roast 1.5 kg

4 Tbsp olive oil 60 mL

2 cups onions 200 g
  cut into chunks

1 cup red pepper 150 g
  cored, seeded, finely diced

1 cup green pepper 150 g
  cored, seeded, finely diced

1 jalapeño pepper 1
  seeded and finely diced

1-2 dried, ancho chillis 1-2
  seeded, and broken into pieces

4 Tbsp minced garlic 60 g

1 cup red wine 250 mL

2 cups roma tomatoes 500 mL
  chopped

2 cups zucchini 240 g
  cut into chunks

1 Tbsp fresh thyme 15 mL

to taste salt and pepper to taste

**6-8 servings**

Combine the spices and rub into the rib roast.

Heat olive oil in a heavy casserole or Dutch oven over high heat until very hot.

Sear the roast on all sides until nicely caramelized. Remove and set aside. Retain the oil.

Preheat oven to 300°F (150°C).

Using the same pan used for searing the beef, add the onions, peppers, and chilies, cooking until the onions are translucent.

Add the garlic and sauté just until its aroma is released.

Deglaze the pan with the red wine.

Add the tomatoes, zucchini, thyme, and season to taste.

Return the rib roast to the pan, cover and braise in the oven for 1 1/2 – 2 hours or until the roast is fork tender.

Serve with basmati rice, couscous, or wrapped in tortillas with salsa, guacamole, and sour cream.

Anne Yarymowich

The Agora at the Art
Gallery of Ontario

"Although both of my parents are of Ukrainian descent, my mother's family settled in Montreal when they emigrated from the Ukraine.

"Tourtière is a classic dish, unique to the French-Canadian culture. There are as many recipes for tourtière as there are cooks who make it. All are highly seasoned and an essential addition to the Christmas table. This recipe is a hybrid of several recipes including my mother's. The addition of rolled oats as a thickener may show a Scottish influence."

# French Canadian Tourtière
## with Pear Cranberry Chutney

½ lb minced onions 227 g

1 oz duck or chicken fat 30 g

1 cinnamon stick 1

3 bay leaves 3

½ tsp ground allspice 2 mL

¼ tsp ground cloves 1 mL

¼ tsp ground cardamom 1 mL

to taste salt and pepper to taste

1 lb ground veal 454 g

1 lb ground pork 454 g

4 oz grated raw potato 110 g

2 oz grated carrot 56 g

2 oz grated parsnip 56 g

⅔ cup rolled oats 80 g
  soaked in 1 bottle of beer 350 mL

½ lb shredded duck confit or
  cooked chicken 227 g

1 cup chicken stock 250 mL

**Pie Dough**

1½ cups all-purpose flour 210 g

½ cup whole wheat flour 70 g

pinch salt pinch

4 oz cold butter 112 g

4 oz cold vegetable shortening 112 g

½ cup + 1 Tbsp ice cold water 140 g

1 egg mixed with
  1 Tbsp water 15 mL

In a large skillet, sweat onion in duck or chicken fat over medium heat until soft and transparent.

Add all the spices, stirring continuously over medium heat for 2 or 3 minutes.

Add veal and pork. Brown the meat well, stirring occasionally with a wooden spoon.

Add potato, carrots, parsnip, oats and duck confit or shredded chicken.

Add chicken stock and bring to a simmer.

Cook at a simmer for 30 minutes, stirring frequently. All the stock should completely evaporate when it is ready.

Taste and adjust seasoning. Tourtière should be highly spiced.

Place filling in a bowl and cool completely by chilling for a minimum of 1 hour.

Pie Dough

Sift flours and salt into a large bowl.

With a cheese grater, grate butter and shortening into the flour.

Work the flour and fat together with fingertips until it resembles oatmeal.

Add water all at once, incorporating with a fork only until dough just comes together. Do not overwork.

Divide dough into 2 pieces.

Shape each piece into a dish. Wrap in plastic.

Refrigerate for 15 minutes.

## Pear Cranberry Chutney

1 large onion 250 g
  finely diced

½ cup cider vinegar 125 g

¼ cup brown sugar 110 g

¼ cup white sugar 100 g

1 tsp salt 7 g

½ tsp cinnamon 2 mL

¼ tsp allspice 1 mL

¼ tsp cracked chili peppers 1 mL

1 lb fresh or frozen whole cranberries
  454 g

1½ lb pears 680 g
  peeled, cored and sliced

1 oz fresh ginger 28 g
  peeled and grated

**8 servings**

Preheat oven to 400°F (200°C).

On a floured surface, roll each disc into a circle of 12-inch (30-cm) diameter.

Line a 10-inch (25-cm) pie plate with one piece of dough.

Fill with chilled meat filling, mounding slightly in the center.

Cover with remaining piece of pastry dough.

Make an egg wash by mixing the egg and water together with a fork.

Brush onto the top of the tourtière. Decorate with pastry scraps if desired.

Bake for 40 minutes. If pastry is browning too quickly, reduce heat to 350°F (180°C) and continue to bake until done.

Let rest 10-20 minutes before serving.

Serve with Pear Cranberry Chutney.


Pear Cranberry Chutney

Place onions, vinegar, sugars and spices into a 12-cup (3-L) non-reactive saucepan.

Bring to a boil.

Add pears, cranberries, and ginger.

Simmer gently for 30 minutes or until fruit is tender and has begun to break down.

Cool and check seasoning.

Serve chilled.

Anne Donnelly

Chef
Arcadian Court

This rich and delicious dish calls for demi-glace, the French classic, a result of prolonged stock making and reduction. It is now available refrigerated or frozen in some high-end gourmet stores. You can also substitute a good, homemade beef stock. If you opt to do this, however, omit the water completely.

# Pork Tenderloin
## with Shiitake Cream Sauce

### Shiitake Cream Sauce

1 Tbsp butter 15 g

½ oz fresh shiitake mushrooms 14 g
finely chopped

2 cups demi-glace 500 mL

1 cup water 250 mL

¾ cup 35% whipping cream 185 mL

1 Tbsp brandy 15 mL

1 Tbsp fresh lemon juice 15 mL

### Assembly

1 16-20 oz pork tenderloin 448-560 g

1 Tbsp + 1 tsp garlic oil 20 mL

1 tsp steak spice 5 mL

½ cup Shiitake Cream Sauce 125 mL

16 baby new potatoes 16
cooked

¼ head broccoli florets ¼ head
cooked

¼ head cauliflower florets ¼ head
cooked

1 zucchini 1
sliced, grilled

4 sprigs rosemary 4 sprigs

**4 servings**

### Shiitake Cream Sauce

In a medium saucepan melt the butter.

Add mushrooms and sauté for 3 minutes.

Add demi-glace, water and cream. Bring to a boil.

Add brandy and lemon juice.

Keep warm over low heat while you prepare the tenderloin.

### Assembly

Brush pork tenderloin pieces all over with oil.

Grill to medium-well done (165°F/72°C).

Sprinkle on all sides with steak spice after initial searing.

Remove from grill and let rest about 10 minutes. Keep warm.

Slice meat on the diagonal.

Place 4 potatoes in the center of each plate.

To the left, place broccoli, cauliflower and zucchini.

Spoon 2 Tbsp (30 mL) of cream sauce per plate along the front of the plate and fan pork slices in the sauce, but resting slightly on the potatoes and vegetables for height.

Garnish each plate with rosemary sprig.

Serve immediately.

Linda Haynes
Ace Bakery

"Try serving the chicken with a baby lettuce and tomato salad. You can also add pieces of peppers or zucchini to the kabobs. For a more substantial dinner, I also like to serve them with a vegetable sauté."

# Marinated Chicken, Pearl Onion and Bread Kabobs

16-20 red or white pearl onions 454 g

5 Tbsp fresh sage, oregano, thyme or
rosemary 75 mL
combined and chopped

1 clove garlic 5 g
chopped

2 Tbsp fresh lemon juice 30 mL

½ cup olive oil 125 mL

3-4 chicken breasts 575 g
skinless, boneless cut into
1 ½-inch (2.5-cm) cubes

12 cubes rustic bread 12
cut into 1-inch (2.5-cm) pieces

5-6 stalks fresh rosemary, thyme or
tarragon 5-6

to taste salt and pepper to taste

8, 8-inch wooden skewers 8, 20-cm
soaked in water

**4 servings**

Preheat oven to 400°F (200°C), or turn on outdoor grill, if using.

Place the onions, skin on, in boiling water for about 4 minutes or until just barely cooked.

Drain and cool the onions. Peel off the skin.

Mix together the chopped herbs, garlic, lemon juice and olive oil.

Pour marinade over the chicken breasts and marinate for 30 minutes to an hour.

Make the kabobs by sliding alternating pieces of chicken, pearl onion and bread cubes onto the wooden skewers.

Insert sprigs of the fresh herb stalks between the alternating layers of chicken, onions and bread.

Brush each skewer with marinade. Season with salt and pepper.

Sear kabobs briefly on a hot grill, turning gently.

Place on baking pan and bake for 10 minutes.

Cover loosely with foil and let rest for 5 minutes before serving.

Lynn Mendelson
Caterer

"This is a modified version of my favorite food in all the world. It is served at Vanipha Lanna, my favorite Thai restaurant in Toronto. They wrap a more complicated version of this recipe in banana leaves and grill on the barbecue. On the side they serve a spicy ping gai sauce. Red curry paste, kaffir lime leaves and fried garlic are available in most Asian markets. If you want to make your own fried garlic, slice 2 cloves of garlic very thin and fry in oil until golden brown. Drain on paper towels."

# Laotian Curried Chicken with Rice

1 Tbsp minced garlic 15 g

¼ cup vegetable oil 65 mL

1 tsp red curry paste 5 mL

2 lbs whole chicken breasts 1 kg
skinless, boneless, cut into strips

2 tsp Chinese curry powder 10 mL

1 red pepper 200 g
cored, seeded, diced

1, 15-oz can baby corn 420 mL
drained and rinsed well

1 cup snow peas 175 g
sliced in half on the diagonal

2 Tbsp oyster sauce 30 mL

1 ½ tsp lime juice 7 mL

½ tsp salt 3 g

3 cups cooked white rice 180 g

5 kaffir lime leaves 5
sliced very thinly

4 green onions 100 g
slivered very thinly

5 sprigs cilantro 5 sprigs

2 Tbsp fried garlic 30 mL

**4 servings**

In a large skillet on medium high heat, fry garlic in oil until light brown.

Reduce heat to medium and add the red curry paste. Stir for 3 minutes, blending paste with oil and garlic. Do not burn.

Add chicken strips to the skillet and stir-fry for 1 minute.

Sprinkle curry powder over chicken and continue to stir-fry until meat turns opaque.

Add red pepper, baby corn, snow peas and oyster sauce.

Stir until sauce thickens and chicken is completely cooked, 12-15 minutes.

Remove skillet from heat and add lime juice and salt.

In a large bowl, mix together the rice, chicken and vegetables, kaffir lime leaves and green onions.

Garnish with fresh cilantro and fried garlic.

Paula Bambrick

**Loblaws Cooking Schools**

"Former baker and kitchen manager at Dufflet Pastries, I now operate my own catering and food consulting business, Personal Chef. This recipe was originally developed for a private client who was dealing with cancer. She had a craving for chili but the various medications she was taking made it difficult for her to digest beef. So I created this version using chicken and she and her kids loved it.

"The recipe has evolved over the years—I have added more spice and coriander cream as garnish. Popular with my family as well as my clients, of all the recipes I have taught, this is without doubt the favourite."

# Chicken Chili with Coriander Cream

2 Tbsp vegetable oil 30 mL

1 lb lean ground chicken or turkey 454 g

2 onions 300 g
chopped

1-2 jalapeño peppers 1-2
minced

4 cloves garlic 15 g
minced

1 Tbsp whole cumin seeds 15 mL

1-2 Tbsp chili powder 15-30 mL

¼ tsp cinnamon 1 mL

½ tsp salt 3 mL

2 roasted red peppers 400 g
coarsely chopped

1, 15-oz can tomatoes 420 g
chopped

1, 15-oz can white kidney beans 420 g

1 cup chicken stock 250 mL

1 cup corn 200 g
fresh, frozen or canned, drained

1 Tbsp fresh oregano 15 mL
or ½ tsp (2 mL) dry

1-2 Tbsp lime juice 15-30 mL
freshly squeezed

to taste salt and pepper to taste

### Coriander Cream

1 cup sour cream 250 mL

½ cup fresh coriander 125 mL
chopped

1 Tbsp freshly squeezed lime juice
15 mL

¼-½ tsp salt 1-2 mL

Heat the oil in a large skillet over medium high heat.

Add chicken or turkey and cook, stirring constantly until it begins to brown.

Add onions and continue to cook until soft and the meat is nicely browned, 5-7 minutes.

Add the jalapeño peppers, garlic, cumin seeds, chili powder, cinnamon and salt and continue to cook for another 2 minutes or so.

Add roasted red peppers, tomatoes, kidney beans and chicken stock and bring to a boil.

Reduce the heat to maintain a simmer and cook until the mixture has thickened slightly, 20-30 minutes. Add the corn and oregano and cook for another 5 minutes.

Taste and add lime juice. Adjust salt and pepper.

Serve with Coriander Cream.

### Coriander Cream

Combine all the ingredients and mix well.

Store in the fridge for up to 2 days.

**4 servings**

Lisa Slater

Co-Founder
Eat to the Beat /
Whole Foods
Market

Once you make this, you won't ever order in or go out for a chicken dinner again. While the instructions are detailed, the preparation is not. Make it once and you won't need the recipe again. All you are doing is roasting a chicken, making a warm dressing from the drippings, and tossing croutons crisped with chicken fat with currants and peppery salad greens and serving the carved chicken on top. A nice bottle of chilled and crisp white wine is all you need to set you on a hillside in Tuscany—or wherever—at a fraction of the cost!

# Tuscan Roast Chicken
## and Bread Salad with Currants and Pine Nuts

1, 3 lb chicken 1.5 kg

2 sprigs fresh rosemary 2 sprigs
    halved

2 cloves garlic 10 g
    thinly sliced

3 cups focaccia or other rustic bread
    750 mL cut in 1-inch (2.5-cm) cubes

3 Tbsp white wine or chicken stock
    45 mL

2 Tbsp shallots 30 g
    diced

3 Tbsp balsamic vinegar 45 mL

1 Tbsp red wine vinegar 15 mL

2 Tbsp dried currants 35 g
    soaked in 1 Tbsp (15 mL) water

¼ cup–½ cup retained chicken fat
    from pan or olive oil 60 mL–125 mL

2 bunches clean arugula, baby spinach
    or mixed greens 2 bunches

to taste salt and pepper to taste

2 Tbsp toasted pine nuts 30 g

**4 servings**

Preheat oven to 400°F (200°C).

Place chicken, breast side up, on a roasting pan.

Gently loosen the skin on the breast by inserting your fingers between the skin and the flesh. Wiggle your fingers around to the thigh and loosen the skin there as well.

Insert sprigs of rosemary and pieces of garlic under the skin of the thigh, leg and breast.

Place the chicken in the oven and roast for approximately 40 minutes or until the juices run clear.

Remove from the oven and proceed with the recipe below.

Remove chicken from oven and place on a cutting board. Cover with foil.

Reduce the oven temperature to 300°F (150°C).

Place the roasting pan on the stove and tilt to one end so that fat and pan juices accumulate in one corner. Use a spoon to skim off all but 4 Tbsp (60 mL) of the fat. Set the fat aside but keep the roasting pan on the stove.

Place the bread cubes in a separate roasting pan. Sprinkle with 2 Tbsp (30 mL) chicken fat set aside, toss, and place in the oven. Set the timer to 8 minutes.

From time to time, check on croutons and toss them to expose all sides to the heat. Reset timer for an additional 3-5 minutes to make them crispy and golden but not dry. Remove them from the oven when ready.

Turn on the heat under the roasting pan on the stove and add the shallots and cook until soft, about 3 minutes. Add the white wine or chicken stock to the pan, scraping up the crispy brown bits and blending them into the liquid to deglaze the pan.

Boil for 1 minute or until the sauce is slightly reduced and thickened.

Add both vinegars and the currants and their liquid to the roasting pan. Boil for 1 minute to reduce further. Taste. If the sauce tastes too strongly of vinegar, dilute with a bit of water or stock. Taste again and season with salt.

Reduce the heat to low and add the reserved chicken fat or olive oil. Whisk to emulsify. Taste. Season with salt and pepper.

Place the washed greens and the croutons on a large, oval platter.

Pour the dressing over the salad, add the pine nuts and toss.

Carve the chicken into 8 pieces (retain the carcass for chicken stock!). Pour any juice from the chicken over the salad. Arrange chicken pieces on top of the salad and serve immediately.

Esther Benaim
**Great Cooks &
The T Spot**

"I grew up with this traditional Moroccan dish. It is true comfort food for me and recently, I was asked to prepare it on *Christine Cushing Live*. Many people have cooked it since then."

# Chicken Tagine

½ tsp salt 2 mL

¼ tsp ground pepper 1 mL

2 tsp ground cumin 10 mL

1, 3 lb chicken 1.5 kg
   cut into 8 pieces

½ lb pitted prunes 227 g

2-3 tsp ground cinnamon 10-15 mL

2 large, onions 500 g
   sliced

1 tsp ground turmeric 5 mL

pinch saffron pinch

1 tsp ground ginger 5 mL

a few pinches salt and pepper
   a few pinches

1 cup whole, blanched almonds 160 g

2 Tbsp vegetable oil 30 mL

toasted sesame seeds toasted
   optional

**4 servings**

In a small bowl, mix together the salt, pepper and cumin. Rub into the skin of the chicken pieces on all sides. Set aside in the fridge for 1 hour.

Meanwhile, in a small saucepan, toss the prunes with the cinnamon and barely cover with cold water. Bring to a boil, reduce heat, and simmer for 10-30 minutes, depending upon the dryness of the prunes, until soft but not falling apart.

In a heavy-bottomed casserole, place the onions, turmeric, saffron, ginger, a few pinches salt and pepper, and 1/2 cup (125 mL) water.

Bring to a boil, reduce the heat, cover, and steam for 15 minutes.

Meanwhile, in a medium saucepan over medium heat, place 1 Tbsp (15 mL) vegetable oil. When the oil is hot, add the almonds and brown. Use a slotted spoon to remove the nuts. Drain on a paper towel. Set aside.

To the same saucepan, using the same oil, add the chicken pieces and brown on all sides over medium heat. As each piece becomes brown, add it to the steamed onions in the casserole.

When all the chicken is in the casserole, add 1 cup (250 mL) water. Cover and simmer on the stove for 30 minutes.

Add the cooked prunes with some or all of their water depending upon how much sauce there is on the chicken. If it looks dry, add all the water.

Continue to cook until the chicken and the prunes are very tender.

When ready to serve, sprinkle the almonds and the sesame seeds over the chicken either placed on a serving dish or right out of the casserole.

Elaina Asselin
**Whole Foods Market**

This recipe looks deceptive. There's nothing special about the ingredients, nor about the technique. But don't be deceived! It is one of the most delicious recipes in the book and achieved with a minimum of effort. You may, as I did, have a lot of sauce left over, but don't worry. Use it to cook your next batch of risotto!

# Chicken with Fennel and Tomatoes

4 chicken legs, thigh and drumstick 800 g
  separated

1 Tbsp olive oil 15 mL

4 cloves garlic 20 g

1 large sweet onion 250 g
  sliced thin

1 fennel bulb 400 g
  sliced thin

4 tomatoes 1 kg
  chopped

1 cup dry white wine 250 mL

1 sprig fresh thyme 1 sprig

1 bay leaf 1

1 generous pinch crumbled saffron
  1 generous pinch

2 cups chicken stock 500 mL

to taste salt and pepper to taste

**4 servings**

Season chicken with salt and pepper.

Heat olive oil in medium saucepan until hot.

Sauté chicken pieces until golden brown all over. Remove and set aside. Reduce heat.

Add garlic, onion, and fennel and sweat until they are translucent but not brown.

Add tomatoes and white wine. Bring to a boil. Return chicken to the pan.

Add the thyme, bay leaf, and saffron.

Add just enough chicken stock to cover. Bring to a simmer and cook until the chicken is done, 15-20 minutes.

Serve with lots of warm, crusty bread to sop up the delicious sauce!

Anne Donnelly
Chef
Arcadian Court

Often, a chef will assemble a great dish from items that are being used in other dishes such as wild rice, for example. Or, they have to make each item in the recipe from what are sometimes called sub-recipes. In this case, you will have to make some wild rice (simmer 8 oz / 225 g wild rice, covered with water until tender. Drain), and some sautéed wild mushrooms (sauté 4 oz / 110 g chopped mushrooms in melted butter until limp and liquid has evaporated) before proceeding to the final assembly. If desired, sauté some julienned vegetables in butter, seasoned with salt and pepper, to complete the dish.

# Salmon in Phyllo

4, 6 oz  salmon fillets 4, 165 g

4 Tbsp clarified butter or oil 60 mL

8 oz wild rice 225 g
    cooked

4 oz wild mushrooms 110 g
    sautéed

to taste salt and pepper to taste

12 sheets phyllo 12 sheets

fresh dill

lemon slices

cooked, julienned vegetables

**4 servings**

Preheat oven to 350°F (180°C).

Place salmon on a baking sheet and cook in the oven for 7-9 minutes only. Increase oven temperature to 400°F (200°C).

Place a piece of wax paper on the counter.

Place 1 piece of phyllo on the waxed paper.

Brush liberally with butter. Repeat using 3 sheets of phyllo per serving.

Place one quarter of the cooked rice in the center of the pastry.

Top with one quarter of the cooked mushrooms.

Lay salmon on top of the mushrooms.

Bring all corners of the phyllo up over the center and pinch together to secure.

Brush the exterior of the phyllo with butter.

Place the salmon in phyllo on a baking sheet covered with parchment paper and cover with foil.

Bake 20 minutes.

Remove the foil and bake until phyllo is golden brown.

Serve on a bed of julienned, sautéed vegetables garnished with a sprig of dill and a slice of lemon.

"This entrée is easy to prepare and spans all seasons. The salmon is also delicious if grilled instead of oven-roasted. The cabbage component is not a soggy, mushy mass à la boiled corned beef and cabbage, but instead is a light, just-softened dish lightened with the addition of wine and lemon."

# Oven-Roasted Salmon
## with Maple Mustard Glaze and Pancetta Braised Cabbage

6, 6 oz fresh salmon fillets 170 g each
  thoroughly de-boned

to taste salt and pepper to taste

2 Tbsp coarse-grained mustard 30 mL

2 Tbsp maple syrup 30 mL

2 green onions 50 g
  chopped

1 tsp fresh tarragon 5 mL
  chopped

3 slices bacon 75 g
  diced

2 shallots 2
  chopped

⅓ head Savoy cabbage ⅓ head
  thinly sliced

½ cup white wine 125 ml

2 Tbsp lemon juice 30 mL

2 Tbsp honey 30 mL

1 tsp fresh thyme 5 mL
  chopped

to taste salt and pepper to taste

6 servings

Preheat oven to 375°F (190°C).

Place salmon on a baking sheet lined with foil or parchment paper.

Season with salt and pepper.

In a bowl, stir together mustard, maple syrup, green onions and tarragon. Season to taste and set aside.

Bake salmon for 8 minutes.

Brush fillets generously with mustard glaze and continue baking until fish flakes when touched with a fork (or to desired doneness). Use remaining glaze as a sauce.

Cook the bacon in a large sauté pan over medium high heat.

Remove and drain off some but not all of the fat.

Add shallots and cabbage and toss in pan for 1 minute.

Add white wine, lemon juice, honey and thyme and continue tossing cabbage until just soft, about 4 minutes.

Season to taste.

Joan Monfaredi

**Executive Chef**
**Park Hyatt Hotel**

"This dish has been a top seller for several years. It is simple and quick to prepare, so everyone wins: the person dining and the person cooking!

"The key is in having an absolutely fresh and well-trimmed piece of fish, and searing the fish at a high temperature to achieve a good color."

# Seared Sea Bass

### Sweet Potato

1 large sweet potato 454 g
  cut into 6 wedges

1 Tbsp olive oil 15 mL

2 tsp assorted fresh herbs 10 mL

### Spinach

1 Tbsp shallots 15 mL
  minced

2 cloves garlic 5 g
  minced

1 Tbsp + 1 tsp olive oil 20 mL

½ bunch spinach ½ bunch
  stemmed, cleaned and chopped

### Sea Bass

2, 4 oz black sea bass fillets, skin on
  150-200 g each

to taste salt and pepper to taste

2 Tbsp olive oil 30 mL

to taste salt and pepper to taste

¼ cup aged balsamic vinegar 65 mL
  reduced to 2 Tbsp (30 mL)

### 2 servings

Preheat oven to 400°F (200°C).

Toss sweet potato with olive oil and herbs.

Bake until fork tender, about 20 minutes.

Remove from oven and keep warm.

In a medium sauté pan, sweat shallots and garlic in olive oil.

Add spinach and cook only until it wilts.

Drain excess liquid. Set aside and keep warm.

Season fish with salt and pepper.

In a hot frying pan, heat oil and sear fish skin side down.

Turn fish over and cook until flesh flakes with a fork. It will be quick.

### Assembly

In the center of each serving plate, arrange the roasted sweet potato wedges.

Pile the wilted spinach directly on top.

Place the sea bass on top of the spinach.

Drizzle aged balsamic reduction around the plate.

### Editor's Note

Joan Monfaredi garnishes this dish with julienned tomato pieces, deep-fried rice noodle sticks and deep-fried lotus root slices.

Elaina Asselin
**Whole Foods
Market**

This is another example of Elaina's creative and successful combination of ingredients not usually seen together. The addition of the sweet but tangy Mutsu apples to the rich sea bass is truly inspired.

# Baked Whole Bass

3 Mutsu apples 600 g

2 fennel bulbs 800 g
sliced thinly

1 Vidalia or other sweet onion 250 g
sliced in julienne

8 pieces bacon 200 g
diced

2, 2-lb whole bass, or other white fish
of similar size 2, 1-kg
cleaned inside and scaled outside

to taste salt and pepper to taste

6 bay leaves 6

1 bunch fresh thyme 1 bunch

1 lemon 1
sliced thin

2 Tbsp olive oil 30 mL

2 cups apple cider 500 mL

1 bunch green onions 150 g
whites and greens, thinly sliced

**6 servings**

Preheat oven to 350°F (180°C).

Peel and slice apples. Toss fennel, onions and apples together and place in the bottom of a baking dish large enough to fit both fish.

Sprinkle with the diced bacon.

Season the inside of the bass with salt and pepper. Divide the lemon slices and the herbs between the fish and place inside.

Drizzle the olive oil over both fish.

Pour the apple cider over the entire dish and place uncovered in a preheated oven for approximately 30 minutes or until the flesh of the fish is just opaque and flakes with a fork.

Serve immediately scattered with the sliced green onions.

Chris Cruz
Bar-One

"I love to cook. I used to skip elementary school and stay home, baking pies and cakes. I graduated with honors from George Brown College in Culinary Management and went on to be the Day and Brunch chef at Ellipsis restaurant for 3 years. I've been at Bar-One now for 2 years and every paycheck is a wonderful gift for doing something I love to do. As for Eat to the Beat, I will do it as long as we are welcome!"

# Octopus Stew

2 Tbsp butter 30 g

3 Tbsp garlic 45 g
    puréed

4 Tbsp parsley 60 g

1 bunch scallions 150 g
    chopped

2 large onions 400 g
    diced

½ cup white wine 125 mL

½ cup fresh lemon juice 125 mL

2 Tbsp tomato paste 30 mL

4-6 lb frozen octopus 2-3 kg
    cleaned and cut into large chunks

2 cups water or vegetable stock 500 mL

2 bay leaves 2

4 large Yukon Gold potatoes 2 kg
    cubed

to taste salt and pepper to taste

to taste chili flakes to taste

4 cups cooked rice 1 L

**4 servings**

To a sauté pan, add the butter, garlic, parsley, scallions, and onion.

Sauté until golden brown.

Deglaze the pan with white wine and lemon juice. Add the tomato paste.

Continue to sauté for 5 minutes over medium heat. Add octopus and sauté for an additional 5 minutes.

Add the water or stock and bay leaves.

Simmer for 45 minutes over medium heat.

Add the potatoes and continue to cook until the potatoes are fork tender.

Season with salt and pepper.

Serve over cooked rice.

Virginia Marr

**Executive Chef
Pillar and Post
Niagara-on-
the-Lake**

Many cooks don't like to try something like mussels at home, but do try it because they yield an incredibly tasty dish for incredibly little labor. That's why you see them on so many menus!

# Niagara Falls Pale Ale Steamed PEI Mussels and Smoked Chorizo Sausage
## with Coriander Pesto

**Coriander Pesto**

2 cloves garlic 10 g

½ bunch fresh coriander ½ bunch
   washed, trimmed of stems

1 tsp grated fresh ginger 5 mL

1 fresh chili roasted 1
   peeled, seeded and chopped

¾ cup olive oil 185 mL

1 large shallot 15 g
   diced

1 tsp olive oil 5 mL


1 bottle pale ale 350 mL

3 lbs fresh mussels 1.5 kg

¾ lb chorizo sausage 324 g
   cooked, diced

1 red pepper 200 g
   roasted, peeled, and chopped

1 ear corn 1
   kernels cut off, but retained

to taste salt and pepper to taste


**4 servings**

In the bowl of a food processor fitted with the steel blade, pulse together the garlic, coriander, ginger, and chili until blended.

With the motor running, slowly add the olive oil until a smooth paste is formed. Set aside.

In a deep pot set over high heat, sauté the shallot in 1 tsp (5 mL) olive oil until soft.

Add the mussels and pale ale. Cover the pot and cook for 3 minutes.

Add diced sausage, red pepper, and fresh corn. Cook for an additional 2 minutes.

Place mussels in serving bowls with cooking juices poured over the top.

Drizzle Coriander Pesto over each bowl and serve immediately.

Izabela Kalabis

**Chef**
**Inniskillin Wines**

"I'm always searching for innovative ways of preparing pickerel (I swear that my husband was born with a fishing rod in his hand) and this one has always been a hit. When fiddleheads aren't in season, I like to use asparagus or fresh fava beans."

# Grilled Pickerel, Fiddleheads, and Red Pepper Smoked Bacon Cream

## Bacon Cream

3 thick slices bacon 85 g

1 tsp butter 5 g

1 clove garlic 5 g
  minced

sprig fresh thyme sprig

5 Tbsp sherry 75 mL

⅓ cup chicken stock 85 mL

⅔ cup cream 165 mL

to taste salt and pepper to taste

## Assembly

4, 6 oz pickerel fillets 4, 175 g each

1 Tbsp olive oil 15 mL

to taste coarse sea salt and
  black pepper to taste

1 tsp butter 5 g

1¾ cups fiddleheads 400 g
  cleaned, and blanched

1 red pepper 200 g
  cut in half, seeded, and sliced thinly

to taste salt and pepper to taste

**4 servings**

### Bacon Cream

Melt butter in a saucepan and add bacon. Sauté until golden.

Add garlic, thyme, and sherry.

Sauté for a few minutes before adding stock.

Reduce by half and add cream.

Lower heat and continue simmering for 10 minutes.

Adjust seasoning and pass through a sieve. Set aside.

### Assembly

Preheat a grill or grill pan to medium hot.

Season fillets with salt and pepper and rub with olive oil.

Grill fillets for 2-3 minutes on each side or until just done.

Remove fish from grill and keep warm.

To a medium skillet, add butter and melt over moderate heat.

Add fiddleheads, red pepper, and seasoning.

Increase the heat to high and sauté for a few minutes.

Reduce heat and add Bacon Cream.

Stir until everything is simmering.

Adjust seasoning.

Place pickerel fillets on plates accompanied by the fiddleheads in sauce.

Chris Cruz
Bar-One

Every now and then, you have neither the time nor the appetite to prepare an elaborate meal and yet you want something soul-satisfying. The following two recipes are just that, relying on the wonderfully calming qualities of eggs. The first is quick and assertive, the second takes a bit longer but is soothing. Both are great.

# Scrambled Eggs and Chorizo Sausage

**Goat Cheese**

½ cup goat cheese 125 mL

to taste salt and pepper to taste

**Red Pepper Jelly**

2 cups sugar 400 g

1 cup white vinegar 250 mL

2 Tbsp dried chili flakes 30 mL

8 sweet red peppers 8
    sliced

to taste salt and pepper to taste

**Chipotle Sauce**

1 small can chipotle peppers
    1 small can

2 whole medium tomatoes 2

to taste salt and pepper to taste

2, 8-inch flour tortillas 2, 20-cm

1 Tbsp vegetable oil 15 mL

½ chorizo sausage ½
    cubed

4 eggs 4

chives chopped

to taste salt and pepper to taste

**2 servings**

Goat Cheese

In a food processor, whip goat cheese with salt and pepper until smooth.

Red Pepper Jelly

Combine all ingredients in a large pot and bring to a boil, stirring only until sugar is dissolved.

Continue to boil and reduce until jelly consistency.

Pour into clean jars and store in the refrigerator.

Chipotle Sauce

Combine both ingredients in a food processor and purée until smooth. Pass through a strainer.

Season with salt and pepper.

Assembly

Preheat oven to 250°F (120°C).

Toast tortillas in oven while you prepare the eggs.

In a large non-stick frying pan, heat 1 Tbsp (15 mL) oil and add chorizo. Sauté until crispy.

Add whisked eggs and scramble.

Place scrambled eggs on toasted tortillas. Garnish with whipped cheese, mounds of red pepper jelly and chipotle sauce. Sprinkle with chives.

Editor's Note

Store-bought red pepper jelly may be substituted for homemade. The chipotle sauce will store well for up to a month and is wonderful, although spicy hot, on sandwiches, in stews and barbecue sauce.

Lori & Henri
Feasson
Bonjour Brioche

The wife and husband team of Lori and Henri Feasson have created an unbeatable neighborhood restaurant, pumping out some of the best croissants and baguettes in the city. Lines wait patiently out the door in the rain and cold for the wonderful rustic creations that satisfy hungry customers at breakfast and lunch, such as the flan below.

# Goat Cheese Basil Flan

1 pound frozen puff pastry dough 454 g thawed, rolled to fit 24-inch x 13-inch (60-cm x 33-cm) rectangular flan pan with removable bottom

1 cup sour cream 250 mL

1 cup goat cheese 227g

2 eggs 2

1 bunch fresh basil 1 bunch chopped

8 Tbsp butter 120 g melted

½ pint cherry tomatoes ½ pint

**4 servings**

Roll out puff pastry and place in flan shell.

Trim edges.

Refrigerate for 30 minutes.

Preheat oven to 375°F (190°C).

Meanwhile, mix together the sour cream, goat cheese, eggs, basil and melted butter. Whisk until smooth.

Fill flan with sour cream mixture.

Place tomatoes 2-by-2 in filling.

Sprinkle with salt and pepper.

Bake for approximately 30 minutes or until pastry is golden brown.

# chapter 6

# pizza, pasta, grains & bread

We were seasoned pros. We knew how to run a silent auction, present smashing designer rooms, serve outstanding wine and beer, sell goodie boxes at the end of the night so the chefs wasted nothing and Willow benefited from the added income. We were on a roll. Roy Thomson Hall provided great support and a high-visibility venue. Word was getting around that Eat to the Beat was one of *the* events of Toronto's social season. The best feedback of all was that it was an event that was fun and completely without attitude.

Still, we were still terrified. We knew that anything could go wrong, like the time a woman collapsed and an ambulance had to be called; or when a chef spilled all her soup, or a great painting failed to sell, or the diamond on the ring fell out of its setting or when we ran out of plates … and then, three weeks before Eat to the Beat, the tragedy of September 11, 2001 struck and everything was put into perspective.

We wondered if we should cancel the event out of respect for those who died. Other organizers were calling off their fundraisers. But we reasoned that women (and men) were still being diagnosed with breast cancer and that Willow's work was no less important now than it was before the destruction of the World Trade Center.

We decided to soldier on. It was a risk. We might not sell as many tickets as prior years. Our donors might back away from their commitments. Our chefs might feel odd about participating. Only the first of these worries was realized and we went on, thanks to the incredible generosity of chefs, wineries/breweries, donors and guests, to raise a record amount of money for Willow. We were thrilled for Willow's sake but the joy was mitigated by the shadow of the times.

The recipes in this chapter are comfort recipes, ones that will make you feel good as you make them and as you enjoy them with your loved ones. There's no place like home.

Andrea Damon
Gibson
**Fred's Bread**

"'Fred' was the name of my first car. Steve, my husband, bought it for me. Steve and I have always loved good bread, so starting Fred's Bread was a natural evolution for us. We wanted to make bread with real flavor, bread with character. These qualities are achieved in only one way— sourdough organic natural leaven.

"Pizza Movie Night at our house is a way of limiting and enjoying TV together. Making the pizzas together is a lot of fun and only a little messy."

# Movie Night Pizza

**Dough**

1 cup water 250 mL

3 Tbsp fresh rosemary 45 mL

2 ½ tsp dry yeast 12 mL

¼ cup + 2 Tbsp olive oil 85 mL

2 ¾ cups all-purpose flour 385 g

1 tsp salt 5 mL

**Toppings**

1 Tbsp olive oil 15 mL

1 onion 200 g
   chopped

1 cup mushrooms 100 g
   thinly sliced

1 bunch fresh spinach 1 bunch
   washed, stemmed, chopped

2 cloves garlic 10 g
   minced

2 cups tomato sauce 500 mL

3 oz Parmesan reggiano 85 g
   grated

3 oz old cheddar 85 g
   grated

3 oz mozzarella 85 g
   grated

**4 servings**

Dough

Place water and rosemary in a small saucepan and bring to a boil.

Remove from the heat. Cover and let stand for 30 minutes.

Remove rosemary from the water, and chop it finely. Reserve the water.

Heat the water to approximately 110°F (65°C).

In the bowl of an electric mixer fitted with the dough hook, mix together the yeast and 1 cup (250 mL) of the rosemary water. Stir in the olive oil.

Add the flour and salt.

Mix on medium speed for about 4 minutes or until the dough is smooth and shiny and comes away from the sides of the bowl. Or, knead by hand to the same consistency, about 10 minutes.

Place dough in an oiled bowl and cover with plastic wrap.

Set aside to rise until doubled in size, approximately 1-1/2–2 hours.

In an oiled 10-inch x 15-inch (25-cm x 38-cm) jelly roll pan, press the dough out gently.

Cover with oiled plastic wrap and allow to rise 30 minutes while you prepare the toppings.

Preheat the oven to 400°F (200°C).

Toppings

Place the oil in a large sauté pan. Sauté the onion and mushrooms until they have released their juices, then cook to evaporate them.

Add garlic, then spinach and cook until just wilted.

Spread tomato sauce over the dough.

Spread the cooked vegetables over the tomato sauce.

Sprinkle the cheeses over the vegetables.

Bake for 30 minutes, until crust is golden and crisp.

Let cool for about 10 minutes before slicing.

Bridget Lunn
Private Caterer

"Saturday night at home means comfort food and as little work as possible for the cook. The basic recipe here is Italian peasant food courtesy of an old boyfriend's grandma. I add to it as the larder and inspiration dictate."

# Saturday Night Pasta
## Red, Green and White

1 lb Italian short, dry pasta 454 g
e.g. bowties

¾-1 lb ricotta cheese 375-454 g

¼- ⅓ cup sun-dried tomatoes 50 g
cut in strips

1 bunch broccoli florets 600 g

¼ lb freshly grated Romano,
Parmesan or Asiago cheese 112 g

1 large bunch Italian parsley 1 large
bunch chopped coarsely

1 Tbsp fruity, extra-virgin olive oil
15 mL

to taste sea salt and black pepper
to taste

**4-6 servings**

Bring a heavy 4-quart (4-L) pot of water to a rapid boil.

Meanwhile, place the ricotta cheese in a large pasta bowl with the sun-dried tomatoes.

When the water reaches the boil, add 1 heaping tablespoon (20 g) of salt and the pasta. Stir until the water returns to the boil, then occasionally until the pasta is done.

One minute before the pasta is done, add the broccoli.

Before draining the pasta and broccoli, reserve 1 cup (250 mL) of the pasta water.

Add some of the water to the ricotta and stir until a loose consistency is reached.

Add 1 Tbsp (15 mL) olive oil or to taste.

Add the pasta and broccoli.

Top with parsley, some of the grated cheese, salt and pepper and toss to combine.

Serve with remaining grated cheese on the side and additional ground pepper at the table.

All chefs have their favorite comfort food. Peller Estates Winery Executive Chef, Jason Rosso, has this favorite recipe courtesy of his grandmother. It will be yours, too. The title is a bit misleading; it's the cheddar that's five years old, not the sauce!

# Macaroni and Cheese
## with 5-Year-Old Cheddar Sauce

3 Tbsp butter 45 g

1 medium onion 200 g
diced

¼ tsp ground nutmeg 1 mL

1 Tbsp garlic purée 15 mL

½ tsp dry mustard 2 mL

3 Tbsp flour 25 g

2 ¼ cups milk 565 mL

1 ¼ cups 35% whipping cream
315 mL

4 cups 5-year-old cheddar 480 g
grated

to taste salt and pepper to taste

### Crust

2 Tbsp roasted garlic purée 30 mL

2 cups egg bread crumbs 260 g

2 Tbsp fresh herbs 30 mL
finely chopped

½ cup grated cheddar 60 g

### Assembly

2 lbs elbow macaroni 1 kg

4 servings

In a large saucepan on medium heat, melt the butter and add the onion, nutmeg, garlic, and mustard powder. Cook for about 3 minutes stirring occasionally.

Add flour and cook for another 2 minutes stirring constantly.

Slowly add milk and then cream, whisking to smooth out some of the lumps. Bring to a boil and cook for about 4 minutes whisking constantly so the bottom won't burn.

Remove from heat and whisk in the cheddar cheese. Season with salt and pepper to taste.

Strain the sauce into another saucepan and set aside while you cook the pasta.

### Crust

Combine all the ingredients for the crust and mix well.

### Assembly

Cook the pasta in lightly salted water to the al dente stage. Drain.

Meanwhile, turn the oven to broil.

Return the saucepan with the cheddar sauce to the stove and bring to a boil, whisking constantly.

Add the macaroni and stir to coat the noodles well. Season to taste.

Pour the macaroni and cheese into a buttered casserole dish. Sprinkle the crust evenly over the top.

Place the casserole in the oven and keep a close eye on it. The breadcrumbs will start to turn brown immediately. When the top is golden, serve and be very happy!

Peller Estates Winery Executive Chef Jason Rosso provided this recipe from his grandmother. It calls for homemade pasta dough. It's nice to think about doing it, but in reality, not many of us have the time or the staff, let alone the energy, to actually make it. So substitute fresh pasta sheets instead which you can purchase at most supermarkets and food shops. Spread filling in a single mound along the bottom edge and roll into a tube, like cannelloni. Place in a gratin dish. Continue until the filling is all used up. Pour the sauce over the top and bake in a 350°F (180°C) oven until bubbly.

# Braised Veal Shank Agnolotti
## with Sweet Mustard Cream

### Filling

1 lb veal shank 454 g

1 cup carrot 227 g
   chopped

1 cup celery 227 g
   chopped

1 ½ cups onions 227 g
   chopped

1 bunch fresh thyme 1 bunch

3 sprigs fresh rosemary 3 sprigs

6 quarts veal stock or beef bouillon 6 L

1 ½ cups chopped fresh herbs 375 mL

to taste chopped garlic to taste

to taste salt and pepper to taste

as needed 35% whipping cream
   as needed

### Pasta Dough

1 cup + 6 Tbsp semolina flour 200 g

1 cup + 6 Tbsp all-purpose flour 200 g

1 tsp salt 5 mL

1 egg 50 g

2 Tbsp olive oil 30 mL

½ cup water 125 mL
   or as needed

### Filling

Preheat oven to 350°F (180°C).

In a large pot set on high heat, season and sear the veal shanks until evenly browned.

Remove veal from the pot and add carrots, celery, and onions. Sauté until brown and caramelized.

Return the veal to the pot and add the thyme, rosemary, and stock or bouillon.

Cover loosely with foil and braise in the oven for about 2 hours.

Remove the veal shanks from the liquid and while still warm, separate the meat from the bones, being sure to remove most of the fat and cartilage.

Chop the meat finely and combine with the fresh herbs, chopped garlic, salt, and pepper.

Mix until well combined and add a little cream to keep the mixture moist. Set aside while you prepare the pasta and the sauce.

### Pasta Dough

In the bowl of a mixer fitted with the dough hook, combine the dry ingredients.

Lightly whisk together the egg and olive oil and add to the dry ingredients, mixing on medium speed.

Add water in small amounts until all the dry ingredients are combined into a smooth ball of dough. It shouldn't be too stiff nor too dry.

Continue to knead the dough for 2-3 minutes.

Wrap in plastic and chill for at least 1 hour prior to using.

### Sweet Mustard Sauce

2 Tbsp butter 30 g

1 ½ cups finely diced onion 200 g

2 cloves minced garlic 10 g

1 cup white wine 250 mL

6 Tbsp honey 90 mL

½ cup grainy mustard 125 mL

1 quart 35% whipping cream 1 L

6 sprigs thyme 6 sprigs

to taste salt and pepper to taste

**6 servings**

Sweet Mustard Sauce

In a medium saucepan, melt butter and sweat onions and garlic until soft and translucent.

Add wine and reduce until most of the wine has evaporated.

Add honey and mustard.

Add cream and thyme and reduce by half.

Remove the thyme and season to taste.

Keep warm over very low heat as you prepare the agnolotti.

Assembly

Roll out the pasta dough to 1/8 inch (.3cm) thick.

Cut out 4-inch (10-cm) circles and set aside under a damp towel.

Spoon 1 Tbsp (15 mL) of veal mixture into the center of each pasta round.

Brush the edges with a little egg wash and fold over to make a half moon shape.

Dab the tips of the half moon with egg wash and fold down to meet each other, forming a crescent. Pinch the edges together to seal into the agnolotti shape.

Keep agnolotti under a damp towel until ready to cook.

Boil the pasta for 2-3 minutes in a pot of lightly salted water.

Drain and toss with the mustard sauce.

Serve immediately.

Lili Sullivan
Freelance Chef

This is one of Lili's signature dishes and is her most sought-after recipe.

# Harvest Barley Risotto

2 cups pearl barley 350 g

4 cups water 1 L

1 ½ tsp salt 8 g

2 Tbsp butter 28 g

2 green onions 50 g
finely chopped

1 red pepper 200 g
chopped

1 zucchini 200 g
chopped

1 cup mixed mushrooms 100 g
sliced

½ cup squash 150 g
peeled, diced

2 cloves garlic 10 g
minced

½ cup dry white wine 125 mL

2 ½-3 cups chicken or vegetable
stock 625-750 mL

½ tsp ground black pepper 2 mL

¾ cup corn kernels 125 g
fresh or frozen

½ cup Parmesan cheese 35 g
grated

**4 servings**

In a large stockpot, combine barley with water and 1/2 tsp (3 g) salt. Bring to a boil, and cook over medium high heat, stirring occasionally.

Reduce heat to low. Partially cover and simmer, stirring occasionally, until barley is tender yet firm, about 30 minutes.

Drain off remaining water but do not rinse. Set aside.

In a large frying pan set over medium high heat, melt the butter. When bubbling, add green onions, red pepper, zucchini, mushrooms, squash, and garlic.

Sauté, stirring often, until the onions have softened, 3-4 minutes.

Add wine, most of the stock, remaining 1 tsp (7 g) salt, pepper, and barley. Bring to a boil, stirring often, until barley has a creamy texture, about 10 minutes.

Stir in some of the remaining stock if the mixture appears too thick.

Stir in corn and Parmesan. Heat just long enough to warm up the corn, stirring frequently.

This recipe may be made ahead up to the addition of the Parmesan.

Reheat chilled risotto, adding more stock and wine to moisten and stirring in the Parmesan at the end.

Jan Sherk
Word of Mouth
Cuisine

# Wild Rice Casserole

1 cup washed wild rice 200 g

2 1/2 cups water 625 mL

2 1/2 Tbsp butter 42 g

1/2 cup almond slivers 80 g

3 shallots 30 g
  coarsely chopped

1 clove garlic 5 g
  minced

10 oz oyster mushrooms 280 g
  thinly sliced

1/2 cup 35% whipping cream 125 mL

2 Tbsp cognac 30 mL

1 tsp salt 5 mL

1 orange rind 1
  finely grated

1 Tbsp butter 15 mL
  for topping

**6 servings**

Put rice and water in a medium saucepan over high heat.

Bring to a boil. Reduce heat to very low, cover tightly and cook for 1–1 1/2 hours, until the grains are tender and fluffy.

Meanwhile, melt 2 Tbsp (30 mL) butter over moderate heat.

Sauté the almonds until they just begin to turn golden.

Add chopped shallots, garlic and mushrooms and sauté until the shallots turn transparent. Set aside.

When the rice is cooked, pour off any excess liquid and combine the rice with the almond-mushroom mixture and remaining ingredients. Pour into a casserole dish.

Dot the top with butter.

The dish can be made up to this point and refrigerated.

Bring to room temperature before reheating in a 325°F (160°C) oven.

If cooking immediately, cover tightly and bake for 45 minutes.

Lisa Slater

Co-Founder
Eat to the Beat /
Whole Foods
Market

Like many women chefs, I started baking at an early age. My first culinary recollection is of receiving a Betty Crocker kids' baking set complete with mini pans, cake and frosting mix to turn into a small layer cake. At age seven, I was hooked and for years had to rely on my mother to turn on the oven.

My grandfather owned a series of innovative New York City restaurants, so I was introduced at a very young age to fabulous settings and cuisine. I opened my first restaurant in New York City, called Slotnick's Daughter. It served gourmet coffees, fine sandwiches, and desserts. This recipe is one I developed for great sandwiches.

# Buttermilk Pecan Bread

1 ¼ cups ground fine pecans 160 g

5 ¾ cups + 2 Tbsp all-purpose flour 825 g

1 Tbsp instant yeast 15 mL

1 Tbsp salt 15 g

3 Tbsp + 1 tsp sugar 50 g

1 ¾ cups buttermilk 300 mL room temperature

¼ cup half-and-half cream 65 mL

2 Tbsp melted butter 30 mL

**2 sandwich loaves**

In the bowl of an electric mixer fitted with the paddle attachment, mix the pecans, flour, yeast, salt and sugar.

Mix the buttermilk, half-and-half and melted butter.

On low speed, add to the dry ingredients and mix until a shaggy mass forms.

Turn off the mixer, replace the paddle with the dough hook, and cover the bowl with a tea towel. Let sit for 20 minutes.

Mix the dough until smooth and elastic. It should be slightly tacky but not sticky. It should register no more than 77°F (25°C) on a quick-read thermometer.

Place in a lightly oiled bowl and cover with plastic wrap.

Let rise until double in bulk.

Preheat the oven to 375°F (190°C). Grease 2, 8-inch x 4-inch (20-cm x 10-cm) bread pans with vegetable spray.

Remove dough from bowl and place on work surface. Divide in half.

Let rest 10 minutes.

Gently press each half into an 8-inch x 12-inch (20-cm x 30-cm) rectangle.

Form each into a cylinder shape by folding in thirds, like a business letter, pinching the final seal, and rolling to fit the length of the pan.

Place in the prepared pans.

Spray lightly with vegetable spray and cover lightly with plastic wrap.

Let rise until about 1 inch (2.5 cm) over the edge of the pan, about 40 minutes to an hour.

Remove plastic and brush lightly with water.

Bake for 15 minutes and turn the pan 180°.

Bake for another 10-20 minutes or until the loaves are a deep golden brown and sound hollow when tapped on the bottom. Be careful not to overbake as the nuts will brown easily.

Lisa Beth
Glassman
The Big Goose

"We've been making this side dish since we opened and it shows no sign of slowing down in popularity! Goes well with fish and fowl."

# Mango Couscous

## Mango Dressing

1 mango 1
  peeled, flesh cut from pit

1 tsp dried mint 5 mL

½ cup rice wine vinegar 125 mL

¼ cup canola oil 65 mL

to taste salt and pepper to taste

## Couscous

1 Tbsp vegetable oil 15 mL

1 cup onion 150 g
  finely diced

½ cup chopped, pitted dates 140 g

½ cup chopped dried apricots 80 g

½ cup raisins 80 g

1 Tbsp dried mint 15 mL

2 Tbsp cumin 30 mL

4 cups apple juice 1 L

4 cups uncooked couscous 400 g

4 stalks green onion 100 g
  finely chopped

½ cup red onion 100 g
  finely chopped

1 mango 1
  peeled, flesh cut from pit,
  finely diced

2 stalks celery 150 g
  finely diced

4 servings

### Mango Dressing

In the bowl of a food processor fitted with the steel blade, purée all the ingredients except the oil.

With the motor running, gradually add the oil and blend until emulsified.

Keeps for a week in the fridge.

### Couscous

In a large saucepan set over medium heat, warm the oil.

Add the onions, dates, apricots and raisins, mint and cumin.

When the onions start to sweat, add the apple juice and bring to a light boil.

Stirring constantly, add the couscous slowly until it is completely mixed in with the other ingredients.

Cover and remove from the heat.

Let sit for 5 minutes then turn out of the pot into a bowl fluffing as you go with a fork.

When cooled, add remaining ingredients with as much Mango Dressing as you like.

Virginia Marr

Executive Chef
Pillar and Post
Niagara-on-
the-Lake

This is a wonderful accompaniment to any stew or soup, not to mention scrambled eggs!

# Smoked Bacon Corn Bread

½ cup all-purpose flour 70 g

1 cup corn meal 130 g

1 tsp salt 5 mL

½ tsp baking soda 2 mL

2 tsp baking powder 10 mL

1 cup smoked bacon 25 g
  cooked, diced (5 slices, approx.)

½ tsp cayenne pepper 2 mL

¼ cup parsley 65 mL
  washed, chopped

1 ¼ cup buttermilk 300 mL

2 eggs 2
  beaten

¼ cup olive oil 65 mL

1 cup Parmesan 65 mL
  grated

4 servings

Preheat oven to 350°F (180°C).

Lightly grease an 8-inch x 4-inch (20-cm x 10-cm) loaf pan and sprinkle liberally with corn meal to coat sides and bottom.

Mix flour, corn meal, salt, baking soda, baking powder, bacon, parsley, and cayenne in medium bowl.

In a small bowl, combine buttermilk, eggs and olive oil.

Add to dry ingredients and stir just until blended.

Add the Parmesan cheese and mix.

Pour batter into loaf pan.

Bake until a toothpick tests clean.

Serve warm with a hearty winter stew or soup.

Andrea Damon
Gibson
Fred's Breads

"This is the bread we served at the very first Eat to the Beat. It is still one of my favorites, a little unusual and great for breakfast, afternoon tea or dessert."

# Sweet Foccacia
## with Grapes, Pine Nuts and Wild Honey

4 Tbsp fresh rosemary 60 mL

1 cup water 250 mL

2 ½ tsp yeast 15 mL

2 ¾ cups bread flour 385 g

2 Tbsp sugar 30 g

1 tsp salt 5 mL

¼ cup + 2 Tbsp olive oil 95 mL

½ lb grapes 227 g
    halved

2 oz pine nuts 56 g

¼ cup honey 85 g

**3-4 servings**

Place rosemary and water in a small saucepan and bring to a boil.

Remove from the heat. Cover and let stand for 30 minutes.

Remove rosemary from the water and chop it finely.

Heat the water to approximately 110°F (50°C).

Sprinkle the yeast on top of the warm water. Let stand 5 minutes.

Combine the flour, 1 Tbsp (15 mL) sugar, and salt and mix in the yeasted water and chopped rosemary.

Knead approximately 10 minutes or until the dough is smooth and elastic.

Place in an oiled bowl and cover with plastic wrap.

Set aside to rise until doubled in size, approximately 1 hour.

In an oiled 10-inch x 15-inch (25-cm x 38-cm) jelly roll pan, press the dough out and dimple it with your fingertips. You might have to let the dough rest a bit in order to get it to the far corners of the pan. If you do, cover it for about 5 minutes before continuing.

Scatter grapes and pine nuts over the dough and press lightly.

Cover the dough with an oiled sheet of plastic wrap (alternately, spray lightly with vegetable oil) and let rise until double in size.

Meanwhile, preheat oven to 400°F (200°C).

Remove plastic wrap and sprinkle 1 Tbsp (15 mL) sugar evenly over the dough.

Bake for 15 minutes.

Remove from the oven and drizzle with honey.

Return to the oven for an additional 10-15 minutes or until brown and crispy.

Remove bread from pan and place on a wire rack.

Slice and serve warm.

# chapter 7

# feasts

Year Seven.

Some people think the number seven is lucky, others don't. A month ago, my mother called to tell me that one of our committee members had been diagnosed with breast cancer. She had called Willow and within two hours was on the phone talking to someone who had had the same diagnosis and was there to support her and answer her questions. Two weeks ago, my sister called to tell me that another one of our long-time committee members had also been diagnosed with breast cancer. It is at moments like these that all the worry and effort of all the volunteers over the years are worth it. We, as a group, have experienced heart attacks, divorces, deaths, loss of jobs, the birth of our beautiful mascot Ethan (Randi Hampson's son and Sharon's grandson), recurrences of breast cancer and breast cancer scares. These most recent cases were so very close to home. It is important to get a regular mammogram, to have regular check-ups; in other words, to take care of yourself. It is also important to keep Willow alive doing the critical work it does for cancer patients.

This chapter is one that celebrates life in the form of the feast: Indian, Contemporary, Moroccan and sophisticated Italian. Get ready to spend some rewarding time in the kitchen, with professional results. Share the fruits of your work—not only the food but the moment—with those you love.

Arvinda Chauhan
Cooking Instructor /
Owner / Healthy
Gourmet Indian
Cooking School

# Indian Feast

Pakoras or Bhajias

Green Coriander Chutney

Raita Yogurt Sauce

Tandoori Chicken

Mushroom Pullao

Naan

Kachumber Indian Salad

Indian-Style Rice Pudding
    with Saffron and Nuts

Arvinda is a founding chef of Eat to the Beat, who served a fabulous array of beautiful and very sweet Indian desserts that first year. Since then, more and more people have been introduced to Indian food, not only due to many new and wonderful restaurants, but also thanks to Arvinda's extensive cooking classes held in her home and in places like Loblaws and the LCBO. Her cooking has also been featured in numerous publications, bringing the complex (but not complicated) cooking of India to the home cook.

Here we offer an Indian feast to prepare when you want to impress family and friends and learn some new recipes that you will make over and over again.

*"I love cooking with my family. Getting all the members of the family involved in cooking brings everyone close together and strengthens family relations. During the holiday seasons, our cooking tradition make them memorable."*

# Pakoras or Bhajias
## Deep Fried Chickpea Flour Fritters

### Batter

2 cups baisen chickpea flour* 300 g

½ tsp salt 2 mL
or to taste

¼ tsp chili powder 1 mL

¼ tsp baking powder or soda 1 mL

¾ cup water 195 mL

### Vegetables

1 small potato 200 g
sliced into ¼-inch (.6-cm) rounds

1 small eggplant 200 g
cut into ¼-inch (.6-cm) slices

1 onion 200 g
sliced into ¼-inch (.6-cm) rings

1 green pepper 200 g
seeded and sliced into rings

2-3 florets of broccoli 200 g
about 1 inch (2.5 cm) each

2 cups light vegetable oil 500 mL
for frying

### 4 servings

*You can find chickpea flour in Indian, bulk and health food stores.

### Batter

In a bowl, mix chickpea flour, salt, chili powder, and baking power or soda.

Add water to make a batter of medium thick consistency, not as thin as crepe batter and not as thick as pancake batter.

Mix well and let stand for 3-4 minutes.

### Vegetables

Place the oil in a wok or deep saucepan.

Heat to 350°F (180°C).

Dip prepared vegetables, one by one, into the batter, coating well on all sides.

Carefully drop the dipped vegetables into the hot frying oil, a few at a time, and fry for 4-5 minutes until golden brown on both sides.

Drain on paper towels.

Serve hot or at room temperature accompanied by Green Coriander Chutney.

Arvinda Chauhan

Cooking Instructor /
Owner / Healthy
Gourmet Indian
Cooking School

# Green Coriander Chutney

1 cup fresh coriander leaves 250 mL
chopped

¾ cup fresh mint leaves 185 mL
(optional)

1 apple 1
cut into large cubes

1 tsp lemon juice 5 mL

2 green chilis 2

½ tsp garlic paste 2 mL

½ tsp or to taste salt 2 mL or to taste

½ tsp whole cumin seeds 2 mL

1 medium fresh tomato 1
chopped into cubes

**4 servings**

Put ingredients into blender and blend on high or medium speed until mixture is fine. Serve chilled with Indian appetizers.

Some Indian cooking is known for its fiery qualities. Raita, the cooling yogurt-based sauce that accompanies almost every Indian meal, acts as a soothing antidote. But don't just make it when you are making Indian-inspired dishes: it's great drizzled into soups, dolloped onto potatoes or as an appetizer dip.

# Raita Yogurt Sauce

1 cup plain yogurt 250 mL

¾ cup grated cucumber 75 mL

½ tsp garlic 2 mL
    mashed to a paste

½ tsp ground cumin 2 mL

½ tsp salt 2 mL

¼ tsp ground mustard seeds 1 mL

¼ tsp red chili powder 1 mL

fresh coriander as garnish

In a bowl, mix all the ingredients except coriander leaves. The consistency of the sauce should be thick, not runny.

Garnish with the fresh coriander and a sprinkle of cumin and red chili powder.

Arvinda Chauhan

Cooking Instructor /
Owner / Healthy
Gourmet Indian
Cooking School

"Authentically, the taste of tandoori chicken is achieved through a tandoor clay oven; however, a very good result is obtained by baking in an oven or on the barbecue."

# Tandoori Chicken

1 tsp garlic 5 mL
   mashed into a paste and measured

1 tsp fresh ginger 5 mL
   mashed into a paste

1 tsp ground black pepper or red chili
   powder 5 mL

¼ tsp red food coloring 1 mL
   (optional)

1 tsp or to taste salt 5 mL or to taste

2 Tbsp vinegar 30 mL

2 Tbsp fresh lemon juice 30 mL

1 cup plain yogurt 250 mL

1 tsp finely chopped fresh mint 5 mL

1 3-lb chicken 1.5 kg
   cut into 8 pieces

vegetable oil

lemon wedges

Green Coriander Chutney

Raita Yogurt Sauce

Naan Flatbread

Kachumber Salad

In a bowl large enough to marinate the chicken, blend all the ingredients except chicken.

Add the chicken pieces and toss to coat them well.

Marinate in the fridge overnight.

Preheat the oven to 350°F (180°C).

Place the chicken pieces on a foil- or parchment-lined baking sheet and bake for 25-30 minutes, turning occasionally.

Brush each piece with a little oil and bake an additional 10 minutes until the chicken pieces are dry and well cooked.

Serve with lemon wedges, Green Coriander Chutney, Raita, salad, and Naan.

# Mushroom Pullao

1 cup basmati rice 200 g

1 Tbsp oil or ghee 15 mL

2 cardamom pods 2

2 cinnamon sticks 2

3-4 bay leaves 3-4

1 large onion 200 g
thinly sliced

1 cup mushrooms 100 g
thinly sliced

½ cup frozen peas 60 g
(optional)

1 tsp salt 5 mL
or to taste

1 ½ cups water 375 mL
add extra if necessary

Wash and soak rice in a few changes of water. Set aside for 10-15 minutes.

Wash again in 2 changes of water, strain through a sieve and set aside.

In a heavy-bottomed or non-stick pan, heat oil or ghee on medium heat.

Add spices and bay leaves, sautéing until slightly brown.

Add onions, mushrooms and peas, if using, and stir. Cook for 2-3 minutes.

Gently fold in rice.

Add salt and water.

Cover and cook until all the water has been absorbed, about 15-20 minutes.

Remove from the heat, remove the lid, and fluff the rice gently with a fork.

Replace the lid and let sit for 5 minutes before serving to firm up.

Arvinda Chauhan

Cooking Instructor /
Owner / Healthy
Gourmet Indian
Cooking School

"Traditionally, naan, a leavened bread, is baked in a tandoor clay oven, although it can be baked just as authentically in a conventional home oven."

# Naan

1 cup warm water 250 mL

2 tsp quick-rise yeast 10 mL

4 cups all-purpose flour 560 g

1 tsp salt 5 mL

1 Tbsp sugar 15 mL

½ tsp baking soda 2 mL

1 ¼ cups plain yogurt 310 mL

1 Tbsp oil or ghee 15 mL

sesame or poppy seeds

coriander

Sprinkle the yeast over the warm water and set aside until bubbly, 5-10 minutes.

In a large bowl mix together the flour, salt, sugar and baking soda.

Make a well in the center and add the yogurt, half the oil or ghee, and yeast mixture.

Mix well and then turn out onto a work surface, kneading until the dough is soft and pliable. Add sufficient water to make the dough smooth but not sticky.

Place in a lightly oiled bowl and cover with plastic. Set aside in a warm place until the dough doubles in size (depending upon the room temperature, this could take 4-6 hours).

Set oven to broil.

Punch the dough down and knead again. Allow to rest for 5 minutes, covered with plastic.

Divide dough into 8 pieces. Roll each ball into either a circle or an elongated flatbread.

Place rolled naan on a baking sheet and bake under the broiler on one side until lightly browned with spots.

Remove from the oven and brush with oil or ghee and sprinkle with sesame, or poppy seeds.

Return to the oven and continue to bake until golden brown but still soft.

Serve immediately.

# Kachumber
## Indian Salad

2 tsp lemon or lime juice 10 mL

1 Tbsp vinegar 15 mL

½ tsp sugar 2 mL

½ tsp salt 2 mL

½ tsp cumin powder 2 mL

¼ tsp hot chili powder 1 mL

1 ½ red onions 350 g
   finely chopped or sliced

3 carrots 300 g
   finely cubed or grated

2 firm tomatoes 500 g
   finely cubed or sliced

½ cucumber 50 g
   finely cubed

1 jalapeño chili 1
   finely chopped (optional)

¼ cup fresh coriander leaves 65 mL
   finely chopped

mint leaves to garnish (optional)

Squeeze lemon or limes into a small bowl.

Add vinegar, sugar, salt, cumin powder, and chili powder. Mix well and set aside.

In a large bowl, mix onions, carrots, tomatoes, cucumber, chili, if using, and coriander leaves.

Add dressing mixture and toss well with chopped vegetables.

Chill in refrigerator and garnish with mint before serving. Serve with curries, Indian flatbreads and Tandoori Chicken.

Arvinda Chauhan

Cooking Instructor /
Owner / Healthy
Gourmet Indian
Cooking School

# Indian-Style Rice Pudding
## with Saffron and Nuts

½ cup short-grain rice 100 g

5 cups whole milk or 2%
1 L plus 250 mL

1 can Carnation evaporated milk 1 can

5-6 Tbsp sugar 75-90 g
to taste

¼ tsp saffron 1 mL
(soaked in water or milk)

1 Tbsp almonds 15 mL
finely chopped

1 Tbsp raw pistachio nuts 15 mL
finely chopped

½ tsp ground cardamom seeds 2 mL

½ tsp nutmeg 2 mL
freshly grated

Soak rice 10-15 minutes. Wash in 3 or 4 changes of water.

Drain rice and put in a large heavy-bottomed pot or non-stick pot.

Add milk and bring it to a boil. Reduce the heat to low.

Cook until the rice is done and the pudding is fairly thick, stirring occasionally.

Add sugar and cook for few more minutes.

Add saffron and remove the pudding from the heat and pour into serving dish.

Garnish with chopped almonds and pistachios, cardamom and nutmeg.

Serve warm or chilled. This rice pudding can also be served with main meal.

Renee Foote
Ginger Island Cuisine

# Contemporary Feast

Thai-Inspired Noodles
  with BBQ Shrimp, Chili
  and Coriander Oils

Grilled Pork Tenderloin
  with Sesame Flavors,
  Toasted Barley Risotto
  and Chanterelle Mushrooms

Roasted Pear Strudel with
  Ginger Parfait

When I asked Renee to send me her bio, in typical modesty, she wrote a long accolade to Canada's other regional chefs, not once mentioning herself. She is too modest: one of our finest Canadian chefs, Renee is known for her immense energy and creativity, drawing on inspiration from home and abroad, and wowing diners with her wildly inventive and colorful, three dimensional dishes. She is perhaps best known for her Chocolate Sushi which she sent by taxi to the first Eat to the Beat because that evening she couldn't leave her station at the stove of the Mercer Street Grill. She can now be found catering fabulous events under her company's aegis Ginger Island Cuisine.

Renee Foote
Ginger Island Cuisine

# Thai-Inspired Noodles
## with BBQ Shrimp, Chili and Coriander Oils

### Noodle Sauce

¼ cup fish sauce 65 mL

2 cups coconut milk 500 mL

2 Tbsp curry powder 30 mL

1 tsp cayenne pepper 5 mL

2 tsp rice wine vinegar 10 mL

4 Tbsp tamarind juice 60 mL

3 Tbsp brown sugar 45 mL

### Coriander Oil

1 bunch coriander 30 g
  roots removed

1 cup vegetable oil 250 mL

to taste salt and pepper to taste

### Chili Oil

1 sweet red pepper 250 g

1 bird's eye chili or Thai chili 1

1 cup vegetable oil 250 mL

to taste salt and pepper to taste

### Noodle Sauce

Purée all the ingredients in a blender. You will have more than required for 4 servings but the sauce is great to share with friends or to store in the freezer.

### Coriander Oil

In a pot of boiling water, blanche the coriander until wilted.

Immediately plunge into cold water to stop the cooking and to refresh.

Drain well and squeeze out as much water as possible.

Coarsely chop.

Transfer to a blender and with the motor running, drizzle in the vegetable oil.

Purée until the color of the oil is even and all of the coriander is well puréed.

Season with salt and pepper.

Strain through a coarse sieve and transfer to a serving pitcher or squeeze bottle.

### Chili Oil

Coarsely chop the pepper and the chili.

Place in a blender and, with the motor running, slowly add the oil.

Purée until completely smooth.

Season to taste with salt and pepper.

If you find it is too hot for your taste, adjust the heat with a pinch or so of brown sugar or a few drops of lemon juice.

### Noodles

½ lb package rice or rice stick noodles
227 g

### Shrimp

12 whole 16/20 black tiger shrimp
340 g

4 bamboo skewers 4
soaked in water overnight to
prevent burning

to taste salt and pepper to taste

oil for brushing on grill

### Noodles (continued)

1 Tbsp sesame oil 15 mL

1 Tbsp vegetable oil 15 mL

2 Tbsp fresh, peeled ginger 30 mL
puréed

2 Tbsp garlic 30 mL
puréed

1 bunch gow choy—Asian flowering
chives cut into ½-inch (1.2-cm)
lengths or
½ bunch green onions 75 g
slivered on the bias

1 small carrot 100 g
thinly julienned

½-¾ cups sliced mushrooms such as
shiitake, button or cremini 50-75 g

8-10 pieces baby bok choy or mature
bok choy 8-10
sliced in thin strips

**4 servings**

### Noodles

Soak in cold water until softened. This will take about
20-30 minutes.

Drain. They are now ready for cooking.

### Shrimp

Heat grill or grill pan to maximum heat.

Thread 3 shrimp on each skewer.

Season with salt and pepper.

Lightly brush grill with oil to prevent shrimp from
sticking.

Lay skewers on grill and cook only until shrimp are just
barely turning pink.

Flip the shrimp to the other side.

Allow the shrimp to finish cooking, about 5-7 minutes
total to maintain their best texture. Remove from the
grill and keep in a warm, not hot, place while you
prepare the noodles.

### Noodles (continued)

Heat a sauté pan over medium high heat, just until it is
beginning to smoke.

Add the 2 oils and then the puréed ginger and garlic.

Cook just until they are beginning to brown.

Add the chives (or green onions), carrot, and mushrooms
(and mature bok choy, if using in place of baby bok
choy).

continued

Renee Foote
Ginger Island Cuisine

# Thai-Inspired Noodles with BBQ Shrimp

(continued)

**Noodles**
continued

Toss vegetables lightly to evenly coat with the hot oil.

Add the noodles and approximately 1 cup (250 mL) of the Noodle Sauce. The noodles will begin to wilt with the heat.

Toss gently to mix all together well and when the noodles are soft, add the baby bok choy, if using.

Season with salt and pepper to taste and portion immediately on serving plates. Be both abstract and artistic with this!

Slide the cooked shrimps from the skewers and place around the noodles.

Lightly drizzle the oil over each plate.

Enjoy at once!

# Grilled Pork Tenderloin
## with Sesame Flavors, Toasted Barley Risotto and Chanterelle Mushrooms

¾ cup vegetable oil 185 mL

½ cup sesame oil 125 mL

4, 6 oz pork tenderloin pieces 675 g

**Risotto Barley Packages**

2 cups pearl barley 360 g

2 Tbsp butter 30 mL

1 small red onion 150 g
  diced

2 cups chanterelle mushrooms 200 g
  stems removed, but saved, and tops
  coarsely chopped

2 cloves garlic 10 g
  minced

4-5 cups chicken or mushroom stock
  1 L-1.25 L

2 Tbsp fresh thyme 30 mL
  chopped

to taste salt and pepper to taste

¼ cup Parmesan cheese 15 g
  grated

1 bunch Swiss chard 1 bunch

4 servings

Mix together the 2 oils.

Marinate the pork overnight in the oil, refrigerated.

Risotto Barley Packages

Preheat oven to 350°F (180°C).

Place 1 cup (250 mL) only of barley on a baking sheet and toast until brown and nutty in aroma. Remove from the oven.

In a medium saucepan set over low heat, melt the butter and add the onion, chopped mushrooms, and garlic. Sweat until the onions are transparent and add both the toasted and untoasted barley grains.

Continue to cook, stirring to coat the grains with butter.

Begin to add the stock a little at a time, allowing the barley to absorb almost everything before the next addition. Stir continuously to develop a risotto texture.

Cook all of the barley in this way. More stock may be needed than the amount given in order to achieve a rice-like consistency.

Once the barley is fully cooked, add the fresh thyme and season with salt and pepper to taste.

Add the Parmesan and stir gently.

Transfer to a casserole and let cool.

Bring a pot of salted water to the boil.

Blanch the Swiss chard leaves until wilted.

Remove and plunge into cold water to stop the cooking.

continued

# Grilled Pork Tenderloin (continued)

## Assembly

¼ cup oyster sauce 65 mL

¼ cup sesame seeds 30 g
toasted

1 recipe Barley Risotto packages
1 recipe

2 Tbsp butter 30 g

2 cups chanterelle mushroom 200 g
stems from above

1 cup reduced, strong beef broth or
meat glaze 250 mL

garnish fresh chives thinly sliced

1 oz bourbon 30 mL
(optional)

Lay leaves flat on cloth or paper toweling to completely
dry.

Using a small paring knife, shave off the thick, centre
ribs without cutting through the entire leaf.

Place 1/4–1/2 cup (65-125 mL) of barley risotto in the
center of each leaf and roll one quarter of the way up.
Fold in the left and right sides to create an even rectangular shape. Continue rolling until you have a neat
bundle.

Assembly

Preheat grill or grill pan to very hot, or an oven to
400°F (200°C).

Grill tenderloins to medium doneness or 140°F (60°C)
on a meat thermometer. Overcooking will result in
tough meat so err on the rare to medium side.

As soon as the meat is cooked, brush with oyster sauce
and sprinkle with sesame seeds.

Allow to rest in a warm place.

Steam or microwave risotto packages by placing on a
plate with a little water, covered with microwaveable
plastic wrap.

Over high heat, melt 2 Tbsp (30 mL) butter. Sauté the
coarsely chopped mushrooms seasoned with salt and
pepper. Cook until they release their liquid and the
liquid has evaporated.

**Assembly**
continued

In my opinion, there is nothing like the taste of sautéed chanterelles deglazed with bourbon at the end of the cooking process, so reduce the heat slightly and add the bourbon. Reduce until it is practically all absorbed.

To assemble, cut the risotto packages in half, horizontally.

Place both packages with the barley facing up in the center of the plate.

Arrange the chanterelle mushrooms on top.

Cut the pork tenderloin into 3 pieces, and arrange in a triangle around the risotto packages.

Drizzle the plate with meat broth or glaze and garnish flamboyantly with a long sprig of chive.

# Roasted Pear Strudel
## with Ginger Parfait

4 Bartlett pears 600 g
cut into eighths

12 Tbsp unsalted butter 180 mL

2 Tbsp honey 30 mL

5 sheets phyllo pastry 5 sheets

½ cup white sugar 100 g

¼ cup white cake or bread crumbs
65 g

### Ginger Parfait

½ cup fresh ginger 75 g
peeled and finely chopped

1 cup 35% whipping cream 250 mL
whipped stiff

1 cup 2% plain yogurt 250 mL

6 egg whites 6
separated

1 ½ cups sugar 300 g

6 egg yolks 6
separated

1 cup sugar 200 g

¼ cup water 65 mL

### Assembly

garnish icing sugar, fruit coulis,
candied nuts, or mint

**4 servings**

In an ovenproof pan set over high heat, sauté the pears in 6 Tbsp (90 mL) of the butter until golden brown.

Add the honey and toss, then place the entire pan in oven to continue roasting until the honey caramelizes.

Remove from the oven and transfer the pears, still in the pan, to a wire rack to cool.

Preheat oven to 400°F (200°C).

Meanwhile, over low heat, melt the remaining butter in a small saucepan.

Lay one piece of phyllo on the work surface in front of you, long end facing you.

Brush lightly with butter and sprinkle entire surface lightly with sugar. Layer with the next sheet of phyllo, spread with the butter and sprinkle with the sugar. Repeat until you have all 5 sheets stacked on top of one another.

Sprinkle the breadcrumbs along the lower third of the top sheet.

Place the cooled pears on top of the crumbs.

Fold the sides just over the pears and roll up jelly roll style.

Place a wire rack on a baking pan and place strudel roll on rack.

Bake until it begins to turn an even golden brown, including the bottom, 15-20 minutes.

Remove from the oven and let cool before cutting.

If desired, serve warm by reheating individual servings before transferring to a dessert plate.

**Ginger Parfait**

Blanch the ginger in boiling water. Drain. Bring new pot of water to a boil and blanch again. Repeat.

Fold together the whipped cream and the yogurt. Chill.

In the bowl of a mixer fitted with the whisk attachment, whip the egg whites until frothy and gradually add the 1 1/2 cups (300 g) sugar. Continue to whip until the whites are stiff and glossy but not dry.

Fold into the whipped cream mixture and return to the fridge.

In the bowl of an electric mixer fitted with the whisk attachment, whip the egg yolks, until very light and aerated, or until a ribbon of batter sinks slowly into itself when drizzled overtop.

Meanwhile, mix the 1 cup (200 g) sugar with water in a small saucepan and bring to a high boil.

Continue to cook until the sugar reaches the hard crack stage or 248°F (120°C).

With the mixer running, pour the sugar syrup down the sides of the bowl until it is incorporated into the egg yolks.

Continue to beat until the yolks are completely cool.

Sprinkle the chopped ginger over egg yolks.

In 3 additions, add the whipped cream–egg white mixture by gently folding into the egg yolks with a large rubber spatula or balloon whisk.

Transfer the parfait mixture to a bowl, a loaf pan, or a cylinder mold, depending upon how you want to serve it.

Freeze at least 8 hours or overnight.

continued

# Roasted Pear Strudel (continued)

Assembly

Slice the pear strudel on the bias or in a plain round.

Place on a dessert plate.

Place a scoop of ginger parfait next to the strudel.

Dust with icing sugar, fruit coulis, candied nuts or mint leaves.

Kathy Wazana
La Casablancaise

# Moroccan Diffa

Couscous aux sept légumes
  Seven-Vegetable Couscous

Mourouzyia
  Braised Lamb Shanks
  with Raisins and Almonds

M'tboukha
  Salade Cuite

Grilled Eggplant Salad

Mediterranean Mixed Salad

Swiss Chard Salad

Spicy Carrot Salad

Orange and Olive Salad

Kathy Wazana is one of those women who is diffident about writing about herself. I can understand why: she is simply too busy helping others to think about herself.

She is a Renaissance woman.

Born in Morocco and raised in France and Canada, she maintains her ties with her birth country through teaching and writing about its cuisine, a sampling of which is provided below. In addition to raising a family, she has worked tirelessly for peace in the Middle East, produced documentaries on Arab-Israeli relations, and founded a program called Playgrounds for Peace. She puts passion, intelligence, and creativity into everything she focuses on and her focus is single-minded and acute. One day, she might just find the time to open a small Moroccan restaurant where her authentic cooking can be sampled by more than just her wide circle of friends! For now, though, you can content yourself with the following yummy recipes.

Kathy Wazana
La Casablancaise

# Couscous aux sept légumes
## Seven-Vegetable Couscous

### Stew

3 onions 400 g
   sliced

1 lb chicken pieces 454 g

½ tsp saffron 2 mL

1 cinnamon stick 1

1 tsp salt 5 mL

½ tsp pepper 2 mL

4 sprigs each fresh coriander
   and flat-leaf parsley 4 sprigs each

2 cups couscous 400 g

1 Tbsp salt 15 mL

½ tsp freshly ground pepper 2 mL

½ tsp turmeric 2 mL

4 small zucchini 480 g

4 carrots 400 g

4 small eggplant 500 g

2 tomatoes 500 g

2 red peppers 400 g

1 pepper squash 100 g

4 small white turnips 200 g

1 small cabbage 400 g
   (optional)

½ tsp turmeric 2 mL

½ tsp cumin 2 mL

8 cloves 8

½ tsp red hot pepper 2 mL
   (optional)

### The Night Before

Prepare a broth: Quarter one of the onions and place in a soup or stock pot with chicken pieces, saffron, cinnamon stick, salt, pepper, parsley, coriander and 8 cups (2 L) of water.

Bring to a boil, then reduce heat, cover and simmer 1 1/2–2 hours.

Let cool, then strain the broth, and keep refrigerated overnight.

Before using, skim the fat off the top and use the clear, fragrant broth as a base for cooking the stew.

Prepare the couscous for steaming (can also be done in advance): Rinse the couscous in cold water in a wide, shallow pan, stirring the grains.

Tip bowl to drain off as much water as you can. Let couscous sit and absorb the remaining water (at least 1/2 hour, preferably longer). It will swell to at least double its volume and become dry and hard.

Fluff up and separate the couscous with a fork. You can also rub it between your fingers or the palms of your hands to make sure you break up all the clumps.

Add salt, fresh ground pepper, turmeric. Mix well.

Meanwhile, prepare the vegetables: clean the zucchini, scrape the carrots, and cut both lengthwise, then into 2–1/2-inch (5-cm) pieces.

Keep stem on the eggplant, then cut lengthwise into 2 pieces.

Peel, seed and quarter the tomato.

Seed and slice red pepper.

2 bay leaves 2

1 Tbsp olive oil 15 mL

1, 15-oz can chickpeas 420 mL
    drained

1 Tbsp brown sugar 15 g

½ tsp cinnamon 2 mL

1 Tbsp butter 15 g

3 Tbsp chopped coriander 45 mL

2 Tbsp salt 30 mL

½ tsp pepper 1 mL

**4 servings**

Halve pepper squash, remove seeds, clean and set aside.

Peel and cut turnips into 2-inch (5-cm) chunks. If using, cut small cabbage into 6 sections, cutting each section with a piece of the stem to hold it together.

The Next Day

Using a large stockpot or bottom part of a couscoussier, lightly sauté 2 sliced onions in 1 Tbsp (15 mL) olive oil.

Add all spices, hot pepper, bay leaves, salt, and pepper. Blend well, continuing to sauté for a few minutes.

Add prepared chicken broth. Bring to a boil. Add tomatoes, cabbage, carrots, and turnips.

Place couscous steamer on top of vegetable stew and seal tightly.

When steam begins to appear through the steamer holes, pour in half the couscous.

Steam 5 minutes then add remaining couscous. Reduce heat and steam 15 minutes.

Remove steamer and dump the couscous back in the wide, shallow pan.

Sprinkle with 3/4 cup (185 mL) cold water.

Wait 15-20 minutes, until water is absorbed and the grain begins to dry again.

Separate and fluff the grains again.

Let cool a few minutes then add oil and mix well to coat all the grains. (This can be done well in advance and couscous can be kept at room temperature, covered with a clean cloth, for several hours.)

continued

# Couscous aux sept légumes (continued)

Add red pepper, eggplant, zucchini, chopped parsley and coriander leaves, and 1 can of drained chickpeas to the broth.

Cook for 30 minutes. Check and adjust seasoning of the broth. If vegetables are cooked and seasoned to taste and broth is reduced to required amount, set aside and keep warm until ready to serve.

Cook pepper squash separately: cut into 6 sections, sprinkle with brown sugar, cinnamon, and butter.

Wrap with foil, making a tent to trap the steam (this will cook the squash much faster and keep it moist). Bake until tender. When ready to serve, moisten with couscous broth.

Second and final steaming

About 1/2 hour before serving, place steamer over vegetable broth or over a pot of boiling water. Seal tightly.

Repeat steaming instructions in steps 5-9 using all the couscous.

Assembly

To serve, transfer steamed couscous directly to a large, round, serving platter.

Moisten with broth from the vegetable stew (about 2 cups [500 mL]).

Make a well in the center and fill with vegetables from the stew.

Decorate the crown of couscous with pieces of carrot and zucchini.

If serving with lamb shanks, see directions in the recipe for Mourouzyia.

# Mourouzyia
## Braised Lamb Shanks with Raisins and Almonds

4 large onions 1 kg
  grated

1 Tbsp (heaping) ras-el-hanout* 15 mL

½ tsp ground cinnamon 2 mL

½ tsp chili pepper 2 mL

½ tsp ground ginger 2 mL

¼ tsp (or generous pinch) saffron 1 mL
  crushed or steeped in ⅛ cup
  (30 mL) boiling water

½ tsp ground cumin 2 mL

1 tsp salt 2 mL

¼ tsp pepper 1 mL

2 Tbsp water 30 mL

6 Tbsp olive oil 90 mL

8 lb lamb shanks 4 kg

½ cup raisins 125 mL

½ cup blanched whole almonds 80 g


*Ras-el-hanout is a Moroccan spice blend akin to Indian garam masala. It can be found in Middle Eastern grocery stores.

Preheat oven to 450°F (230°C).

Mix grated onions, spices, oil, salt and pepper and water in a large bowl.

Add lamb shanks and coat well with the mixture.

Transfer to an ovenproof ceramic or earthenware dish with a tight-fitting lid.

Cover and place in the hot oven for 30 minutes, then reduce heat to 275°F (130°C) (250°F [120°C] if using a cast iron dish) and cook for at least 2-3 hours, checking frequently to make sure there is enough liquid and turning shanks over in the sauce.

Meanwhile, fry almonds lightly, until golden. Reserve.

When shanks are falling-off-the-bone tender and onions are reduced to a rich brown sauce, add raisins and return to oven for 5 more minutes. (If the sauce is too thick, add 1/4 cup [65 mL] of water, then add the raisins.)

To serve, make a bed of couscous on each plate. Place one shank in the center of each place. Spoon sauce over the meat and sprinkle with almonds.

Pour some of the spicy broth over meat and couscous.

If making with a seven-vegetable couscous, present the vegetables separately, over a large communal platter of couscous and vegetables.

Kathy Wazana
La Casablancaise

"Often used as a condiment or an accompaniment for cous-cous and other dishes, this savory salad comes from Essaouira, a fishing village on the southern Atlantic coast of Morocco. M'tboukha should have the consistency of a confiture, thick enough to use as a filling for sandwiches. At least one restaurant in Essaouira serves a 'Seafood M'tboukha', adding small shrimp to the salad and cooking for just a few minutes before serving. In my family, we always make sure there is some M'tboukha on the table with the couscous course."

# M'tboukha
## Salade cuite

### Basic recipe

5 Tbsp olive oil 75 mL

4 cloves garlic 20 g
finely chopped

1 tsp sweet paprika or tomato paste
5 mL

2 lbs fresh ripe tomatoes 1 kg
peeled, seeded, chopped

4 green peppers 800 g
roasted, peeled, seeded and cut
into strips

2 hot banana peppers 100 g
or one jalapeño roasted, peeled,
seeded and cut into strips (optional)

to taste salt to taste

Heat 4 Tbsp (60 mL) of oil in a heavy stainless steel pot. Add garlic and heat until just fragrant.

Add paprika or tomato paste and fry without burning.

Add tomatoes. Bring to boil, reduce heat and cook, covered, for 30 minutes.

Check once in a while and mash and stir the mixture.

After 30 minutes, remove lid and cook at a simmer until half the liquid released by the tomatoes has evaporated.

Add peppers; mix and continue to simmer on medium low heat until all liquid has evaporated (at least 1 hour).

Add 1 Tbsp (15 mL) olive oil, raise heat to high and finish evaporating while stirring constantly to prevent sticking.

Remove from heat and cool. Before serving, add a drizzle of oil if the salad looks a little dull. Salt to taste.

### A quick alternative

1 can whole Italian plum tomatoes
280 mL (minus the juice) seeded
and chopped

2 green peppers 400 g
seeded and chopped roughly

3 cloves garlic 15 g
finely chopped

3 Tbsp olive oil 45 mL

to taste salt to taste

to taste chili pepper to taste

The following is a quick version of M'tboukha. The results are good enough to make one think twice about grilling, peeling, and chopping. Try both, and also try a variation of both: i.e. canned tomatoes and grilled peppers, etc.

Put all ingredients in a pot at the same time and cook as above.

# Grilled Eggplant Salad

1 large eggplant 400 g

to taste salt and pepper to taste

¼ cup olive oil 65 mL

2-3 cloves garlic 15 g
  finely minced

½ lemon 25 mL
  juiced

1 small bunch fresh coriander 30 g
  chopped

Slice eggplant crosswise into 1/2-inch (1.2-cm) slices.

Sprinkle with salt and pepper, brush lightly with olive oil, and grill until brown and soft. (Although most recipes recommend salting the eggplant for 1/2 hour to draw out the bitter juices, this is not necessary with very fresh, firm eggplant.)

Immediately place grilled eggplant in a bowl and cover bowl tightly with plastic wrap to allow eggplant to steam and soften.

Combine olive oil, garlic, lemon juice and mix well to make a light dressing.

Once eggplant has cooled, cut into bite-sized pieces, add chopped coriander and toss with dressing.

Kathy Wazana
La Casablancaise

"Every Mediterranean country has laid claim to this recipe. What distinguishes the Moroccan version of this salad, sometimes called Macedonian, Israeli or Middle-Eastern, is the use of preserved lemon and olives. And, while I have called it a Mixed Salad, its Moroccan name is *Salade de Tomates*, as the tomato is the dominant ingredient."

# Mediterranean Mixed Salad

3 tomatoes 750 g
   these should be red, ripe but firm

1 sweet green pepper 200 g

1 small hot pepper 50 g
   (optional)

¼ cucumber 25 g

1 white onion 200 g

2-3 small stalks celery heart 80-100 g

1 Tbsp fresh mint or flat-leaf parsley
   15 mL finely chopped

½ cup chopped fresh coriander
   125 mL

1 preserved lemon 1 or
   2 Tbsp fresh lemon juice 30 mL

½ cup green or sun dried black
   (Moroccan) olives 125 mL
   pitted, and chopped

5 Tbsp olive oil 75 mL

salt

Chop all ingredients into small cubes, keeping tomatoes a little larger than the rest.

Add oil and lemon juice, if using fresh lemon.

Toss and season to taste.

# Swiss Chard Salad

1 bunch Swiss chard 1 bunch
boiled until just tender

2 cloves garlic 10 g
minced

2 Tbsp preserved lemon 30 mL
finely chopped

2 Tbsp fresh lemon juice 30 mL

olive oil

salt and pepper

to taste ground cumin to taste

Chop cooled Swiss chard coarsely.

Mix all other ingredients in large bowl.

Toss in Swiss chard.

Chill for 1 or 2 hours before serving.

Taste should be fresh and slightly tart, to offset strong,
spicy flavors of the other salads.

Kathy Wazana
La Casablancaise

# Spicy Carrot Salad

1 bag baby carrots 350 g

3 whole cloves garlic 15 g
   peeled

1 Tbsp olive oil 30 mL

½ tsp cumin 2mL

½ tsp chili pepper 2mL

1 small bunch fresh coriander 30 g

1 Tbsp lemon juice 15 mL

to taste salt to taste

Boil carrots with garlic cloves and salt until tender. Drain and reserve cooking liquid.

In a skillet or saucepan, heat olive oil; stir in cumin, chili pepper and half the lemon juice. Add carrots and toss well until completely coated with the sauce.

Remove from heat. This salad is best made in advance and left to cool for several hours in the fridge to allow the carrots to absorb all the flavors.

Before serving, mix the coriander with a little more olive oil and the rest of the lemon juice. Toss carrots with this dressing and serve.

# Orange and Olive Salad

4 seedless oranges 800 g

½ cup black sun-dried olives
   (Moroccan olives) 125 mL

½ red onion 125 g
   sliced very thin (optional)

½ tsp chili pepper 2 mL

3 Tbsp olive oil 45 mL

5-6 mint leaves 5-6

1 Tbsp orange flower water 15 mL

2 Tbsp lemon juice 30 mL

Peel oranges, removing all the pith.

Separate into skinless segments, letting all the juice run into the salad bowl.

Add olives and sliced onion to the orange segments and juice.

Mix all other ingredients together and toss into the oranges and olives.

Chill before serving.

# Italian Feast

Prosciutto Wrapped Goat
  Cheese with Glazed Pears

Garlic and Oregano Roasted
  Red Snapper

Corn and Pancetta Risotto
  with a Medley of Mushrooms

Dolce Chocolatto

Ida Pusateri and her family oversee one of Toronto's foremost fancy food stores. Stocked to the rafters with the most wonderful foods from around the world, a visitor can see Ida early in the morning and late into the day, meticulously dressed, watching over every detail of the store. A consummate food professional, nothing misses her keen eye and she is known for her superb palate and reading of the marketplace.

This meal is indicative of contemporary, sophisticated Italian dining and exemplifies Pusateri's ethos of quality, taste, and ease of preparation.

# Prosciutto Wrapped Goat Cheese
## with Glazed Pears

2 pears 300 g
   peeled, halved

1 cup maple syrup 250 mL

to taste cracked black pepper to taste

½ lb goat cheese 227 g
   sliced

8 pieces prosciutto 8 pieces
   sliced

4 tsp olive tapenade 20 mL

4 tsp olive oil 20 mL

4 cups mesclun greens 1 L
   tossed with your favorite dressing

**4 servings**

Preheat oven to 325°F (160°C).

Place pears in a pie dish.

Pour maple syrup over pears and season with pepper.

Roast in the oven for 20-25 minutes or until golden brown.

Remove from the oven. Keep the oven on and set pears aside.

Meanwhile make the parcels.

Spread 1 tsp (5 mL) tapenade over each slice of goat cheese.

Wrap with 2 slices of prosciutto to make a little bundle.

Place in the fridge while the pears bake.

When ready to serve, heat the olive oil in a medium sauté pan over high heat.

Quickly brown the prosciutto bundles on both sides and place on a second pie plate.

Bake for 3 minutes or until just slightly warmed up.

Place 1 cup (250 mL) of dressed greens on each salad plate.

Top with a pear half, cut side up, and a prosciutto bundle.

Serve immediately.

# Garlic and Oregano Roasted Red Snapper

3, 1 ½-2 lb whole red snappers
  3, 750-1 kg

½ red onion 100 g
  sliced into rings

6 sprigs fresh oregano 6 sprigs

6 sprigs fresh thyme 6 sprigs

6 lemon slices 6

¼ cup celery hearts 60 g
  chopped

6 cloves garlic 30 g

to taste salt and cracked pepper
  to taste

½ cup olive oil 125 mL

1 red pepper 200 g
  cut into rings

1 orange pepper 200 g
  cut into rings

1 zucchini 120 g
  cut into thick julienne

for garnish lemon rings,
  fresh oregano sprigs

balsamic vinegar

Preheat oven to 350°F (180°C). Line a roasting pan with parchment paper.

Arrange red onion rings, thyme, lemon, celery, and garlic in layers in the cavity of each fish.

Season with salt and pepper.

Close cavity and drizzle half the olive oil over the fish. Place the fish on the prepared roasting pan.

Season the outside with salt and pepper.

Toss pepper rings and zucchini with remaining oil and season with salt and pepper. Spread over and around the fish on the roasting pan.

Bake for 20-30 minutes.

Remove vegetables from pan and place on a serving platter.

Lay the whole fish on top of the vegetables.

Garnish platter with lemon rings and fresh oregano.

Drizzle with balsamic vinegar before serving.

4 servings

# Corn and Pancetta Risotto
## with a Medley of Mushrooms

½ cup olive oil 125 mL

½ cup shallots 90 g
  minced

1 cup pancetta 225 g
  diced

1 cup fresh corn kernels 250 mL

2 cups arborio rice 400 g

1 bay leaf 1

2 sprigs fresh thyme 2 sprigs

9 cups chicken stock 2.5 L

4 cups mixed mushrooms 400 g
  cut into 1-inch (2.5-cm) pieces

5 Tbsp + 2 tsp butter 80 g

½ cup Parmesan cheese 35 g
  grated

¼ cup green onion 60 g
  sliced

to taste salt and pepper to taste

**4 servings**

In a medium saucepan, heat half the oil. Sweat shallots until soft and translucent.

Add pancetta and corn kernels. Sauté until pancetta is golden brown.

Add arborio rice and stir until rice is coated with olive oil.

Add bay leaf and thyme.

Over medium heat, slowly add chicken stock one ladleful at a time, waiting until the liquid has been absorbed before adding more. Keep stirring.

Meanwhile, in a sauté pan, heat remaining olive oil.

Add diced mushrooms and sauté, stirring occasionally, until golden brown. Set aside.

When rice has cooked al dente, 12-14 minutes, remove from heat.

Stir in butter, Parmesan, and green onion.

Remove bay leaf and thyme sprig.

Season with salt and pepper and serve immediately.

# Dolce Chocolatto

1 lb bittersweet chocolate 454 g
melted, still warm

10 Tbsp butter 140 g
room temperature

4 eggs 4
separated

2 Tbsp flour 18 g

pinch salt pinch

2 Tbsp sugar 30 g

garnish fresh berries, whipped cream

**Serves 4**
with leftovers in square dish

**Serves 6**
in ramekins

Preheat oven to 425°F (210°C).

Prepare an 8-inch (20-cm) square baking dish by lining the bottom with parchment paper or spray 6 individual ramekins with vegetable spray. Set aside.

In a medium bowl, mix chocolate with butter until melted. Let cool.

In the bowl of an electric mixer fitted with the whisk attachment, beat egg yolks until fluffy. On low speed, add flour.

Wash and dry whisk attachment.

In a clean bowl, using the whisk attachment, beat egg whites and salt until the soft peak stage.

Gradually add the sugar and beat until stiff but not dry.

Fold chocolate-butter mixture into egg yolks and mix well.

Add one third of the whites and fold gently. Add remaining whites and fold in completely. Fold until no white streaks are left.

Pour into prepared pan or ramekins.

Bake for exactly 15 minutes. It will look as if it is not cooked but as it cools down, it continues to cook.

When still warm but no longer hot, place a serving dish or individual serving plates on top of the baking dish(es) and invert.

Serve warm, garnished with whipped cream and fresh berries.

# Eat to the Beat History

Eat to the Beat was born almost seven years ago, the brainchild of sisters Lisa and Abigail Slater. As the owners, at that time, of the BakeWorks bakery café chain in Toronto, they were looking for a charitable organization with which to ally their business. They had already collected a penny from every bagel sold in a campaign called PennyWorks, the proceeds designated for a community charity. It wasn't until Abby attended the first Willow fundraising event and heard the heroic stories of breast cancer survivors, including the story of Sharon Hampson of Sharon, Lois & Bram, that she and Lisa decided to focus their charitable efforts on Willow.

Having co-chaired the first Taste of Toronto, Lisa was eager to initiate a similar event, this time focusing on women chefs. Since most women chefs are unsung heroines in the professional kitchen, it was her desire to give women the spotlight.

For the first two years the event was held at Casa Loma and raised about $100,000. For the third year, responding to the increased participation of women chefs and the popularity of the event, the venue of Roy Thomson Hall was selected. Eat to the Beat is now hugely popular, attended annually by between 700 and 900 people. In 2001 it generated over $190,000 for Willow's operating expenses.

Every year, a live swing band called The Advocats, comprised of a group of lawyers, donate their music. Hence the name of the event.

The recent addition of microbreweries and wineries compliments the dazzling array of culinary delights created by a roster of over 40 top female chefs from across Ontario.

There is also a silent auction featuring 125 fantastic items, as well as the Designer Showcase rooms created by some of Toronto's top interior designers.

Eat to the Beat is put on by an incredibly talented and committed group of volunteers who work tirelessly to make this event the success it is. Through their generosity and that of the small business and corporate community, proceeds from Eat to the Beat comprise almost one third of Willow's annual operating budget and help the many people dealing with the devastation of breast cancer who rely on Willow's services and empathy.

# index

## A

# C

# E

# F

# H

# I

# J

# K

# L

# M

# N

# O

# P

# T

# W

# Y

# Z